Gender, Peace and Security in Afr

There is often a moment in time that acts as a rallying point around a particular issue. One of those moments for women, peace and security was in 2015 as numerous landmark anniversaries were celebrated in the field. Africa has, in many ways, been the global laboratory for the gender, peace and security agenda, not only because of the number of conflicts occurring on the continent but also because African regional organisations, governments and civil society organisations have been at the forefront of striving for gender equality and implementing United Nations Security Council Resolution 1325. This book explores gender, peace and security in Africa from multiple angles, including the conceptual and implementation challenges and shifts around women, peace and security in Africa over the last 15 years; women's role as combatants in national liberation forces in South Africa; the dynamics of gender in the military through the lens of Kenyan women combatants; food security through a feminist lens; and a series of case studies on the nexus between gender and security in Zimbabwe, Nigeria, Madagascar, the Democratic Republic of Congo, Kenya and Somalia. This book was previously published as a special issue of the *African Security Review*.

Cheryl Hendricks is a Professor and the Head of the Department of Politics and International Relations at the University of Johannesburg, South Africa. She has worked in the field of gender, peace and security, and security sector governance, for well over a decade. She has worked extensively with civil society organisations on gender and security.

Romi Sigsworth is the Editor of the *African Security Review* and a Gender Specialist at the Institute for Security Studies. She has worked on various gender-related topics in South Africa and on the African continent for a decade.

Gender, Peace and Security in Africa

Edited by
Cheryl Hendricks and Romi Sigsworth

Routledge
Taylor & Francis Group

LONDON AND NEW YORK

First published 2016
by Routledge
2 Park Square, Milton Park, Abingdon, Oxfordshire OX14 4RN
711 Third Avenue, New York, NY 10017

Routledge is an imprint of the Taylor & Francis Group, an informa business

First issued in paperback 2018

Copyright © 2016 Institute for Security Studies

British Library Cataloguing in Publication Data
A catalogue record for this book is available from the British Library

ISBN 13: 978-1-138-69142-1 (hbk)
ISBN 13: 978-0-367-02291-4 (pbk)

Typeset in Bembo
by diacriTech, Chennai

Publisher's Note
The publisher accepts responsibility for any inconsistencies that may have arisen
during the conversion of this book from journal articles to book chapters, namely
the possible inclusion of journal terminology.

Disclaimer
Every effort has been made to contact copyright holders for their permission to
reprint material in this book. The publishers would be grateful to hear from any
copyright holder who is not here acknowledged and will undertake to rectify any
errors or omissions in future editions of this book.

Contents

CONTENTS

Citation Information

The chapters in this book were originally published in the *African Security Review*, volume 24, issue 4 (November 2015). When citing this material, please use the original page numbering for each article, as follows:

Editorial note
Romi Sigsworth and Cheryl Hendricks
African Security Review, volume 24, issue 4 (November 2015) pp. 361–363

Chapter 1
Women, peace and security in Africa: Conceptual and implementation challenges and shifts
Cheryl Hendricks
African Security Review, volume 24, issue 4 (November 2015) pp. 364–375

Chapter 2
The convergence and divergence of three pillars of influence in gender and security
'Funmi Olonisakin, Cheryl Hendricks and Awino Okech
African Security Review, volume 24, issue 4 (November 2015) pp. 376–389

Chapter 3
Women combatants and the liberation movements in South Africa: Guerrilla girls, combative mothers and the in-betweeners
Siphokazi Magadla
African Security Review, volume 24, issue 4 (November 2015) pp. 390–402

Chapter 4
Feminine masculinities in the military: The case of female combatants in the Kenya Defence Forces' operation in Somalia
Mokua Ombati
African Security Review, volume 24, issue 4 (November 2015) pp. 403–413

Chapter 5
Gender, feminism and food studies: A critical review
Desiree Lewis
African Security Review, volume 24, issue 4 (November 2015) pp. 414–429

Chapter 6

A case study of gender and security sector reform in Zimbabwe
Netsai Mushonga
African Security Review, volume 24, issue 4 (November 2015) pp. 430–437

Chapter 7

Women police in the Nigerian security sector
Tosin Akinjobi-Babatunde
African Security Review, volume 24, issue 4 (November 2015) pp. 438–444

Chapter 8

Madagascar: Paving the way to national 'fampihavanana' and lasting peace
Gaby Razafindrakoto
African Security Review, volume 24, issue 4 (November 2015) pp. 445–449

Chapter 9

Sexual and gender-based violence in the Democratic Republic of Congo
Yolanda Sadie
African Security Review, volume 24, issue 4 (November 2015) pp. 450–457

Chapter 10

Kenya and Somalia: Fragile constitutional gains for women and the threat of patriarchy
Hawa Noor Mohammed
African Security Review, volume 24, issue 4 (November 2015) pp. 458–474

For any permission-related enquiries please visit:
http://www.tandfonline.com/page/help/permissions

Notes on Contributors

Tosin Akinjobi-Babatunde is a Lecturer in the Department of History and International Relations at Elizade University, Ondo, Nigeria.

Cheryl Hendricks is a Professor and the Head of the Department of Politics and International Relations at the University of Johannesburg, South Africa.

Desiree Lewis is a Professor in the Women and Gender Studies Department at the University of the Western Cape.

Siphokazi Magadla is a Lecturer in the Political and International Studies Department at Rhodes University, Grahamstown, South Africa.

Netsai Mushonga is an independent development consultant.

Hawa Noor Mohammed is a gender, peace and security researcher based in Nairobi.

Awino Okech is a Senior Research Associate in the Department of Politics at the University of Johannesburg, South Africa.

'Funmi Olonisakin is a Professor of Security, Leadership and Society at Kings College, London. She is also the Founding Director of the African Leadership Centre and a Research Associate in the Department of Political Science at the University of Pretoria, South Africa.

Mokua Ombati is a doctoral candidate and research fellow in the Department of Anthropology and Human Ecology at Moi University, Eldoret, Kenya.

Gaby Razafindrakoto is the Secretary of the Federation for the Promotion of Women and Children, Focal Point of the SADC Gender Protocol Alliance.

Yolanda Sadie is a Professor in the Department of Politics and International Relations at the University of Johannesburg, South Africa.

Romi Sigsworth is the Editor of the *African Security Review* and a Gender Specialist at the Institute for Security Studies.

Introduction

Romi Sigsworth and Cheryl Hendricks

There is often a moment in time that acts as a rallying point around a particular issue. 2015 is one of those moments for women, peace and security.

2015 is the twentieth anniversary of the Beijing Platform for Action, the vision of which was gender equality and the empowerment of women everywhere. The Beijing Platform for Action recognised that '[l]ocal, national, regional and global peace is attainable and is inextricably linked with the advancement of women, who are a fundamental force for leadership, conflict resolution and the promotion of lasting peace at all levels'.[1]

2015 is also the fifteenth anniversary of United Nations Security Council Resolution (UNSCR) 1325, which recognises both the differential impact of war on women and the pivotal role women do and should play in conflict management, conflict resolution, and sustainable peace. The UNSC has commissioned a global study that examined women's role in peace and security over the last 15 years, with inputs from a broad range of stakeholders across the world. In October 2015 the UNSC will convene a high-level review of women, peace and security, drawing on the findings of the global study, to assess progress at the global, regional and national levels in implementing UNSCR 1325 and to chart a new way forward to achieve the participation of women in peace and security sector processes and decision-making and to enhance the security of women.

Africa has been at the coalface of the impact of conflict on women; African regional organisations, African governments and civil society in Africa, particularly women's organisations, have been at the forefront of striving for gender equality and implementing UNSCR 1325. The African Union (AU) declared 2015 as the 'Year of Women's Empowerment and Development towards Africa's Agenda 2063', and the AU has integrated UNSCR 1325 into its gender-related frameworks. 2015 is also the expiry date for commitments made by the Southern African Development Community (SADC) member states on gender equality and empowerment through the SADC Protocol on Gender and Development (2008). Article 28 of the Protocol commits member states to putting 'in place measures to ensure that women have equal representation and participation in key decision-making positions in conflict resolution and peace building processes by 2015 in accordance with United Nations Security Council Resolution 1325 on Women, Peace and Security', as well as protecting women and children caught up in conflict and bringing to justice the perpetrators of such violence.[2] Other regional organisations in Africa, such as the

Economic Community of West African States (ECOWAS) and the Intergovernmental Authority on Development (IGAD) have also adopted National Action Plans (NAPs) for the implementation of UNSCR 1325. Many African countries now have relatively high percentages of women in government and in the security sector; countries such as South Africa, Tanzania, Zimbabwe, Ghana and Nigeria deploy large numbers of women in peacekeeping operations. Many countries have also adopted gender-mainstreaming policies. But the actual empowerment and security of women remains a challenge. There is therefore a need to go back to the drawing board to assess what has worked and where and why the gaps remain.

In this crucial year, this special issue of *African Security Review* is dedicated to the theme of women, peace and security in Africa.

Cheryl Hendricks, the guest editor of this special issue, sets the scene by outlining the conceptual and implementation challenges and shifts around women, peace and security in Africa over the last 15 years. Her article is complemented by an examination of the three pillars of influence in gender and security – feminist security studies, civil society activism and policy decision-making and its role in the adoption and implementation of UNSCR 1325. 'Funmi Olonisakin, Cheryl Hendricks, and Awino Okech argue that these three pillars, individually and collectively, have made important contributions to the debate and action on the gender and security agenda, but that they remain organically disconnected.

Shifting inwards from big-picture analyses, there follow a series of articles that focus on specific areas of the women, peace and security agenda. Siphokazi Magadla examines women's role as combatants in national liberation forces in South Africa. The author introduces three categories – guerrilla girls, combative mothers and the in-betweeners – to theorise about women's combat roles in the anti-apartheid struggle, and uses these categories to broaden and challenge the dominant notions of combat that often hide women's contributions in war. Mokua Ombati explores the dynamics of gender in the military through the lens of Kenyan women combatants in the war against al-Shabaab insurgents in Somalia. Ombati argues that it is not sufficient to merely include women in the military, but that there is a need to challenge the continued ideological foundation of militaries and their reproduction of male dominance. Desiree Lewis looks at food security through a feminist lens, by offering a critical assessment of what food security studies has entailed at the regional level and in global terms. She also focuses on the methodological and theoretical feminist interventions that can stimulate rigorous conceptual and research shifts in, as well as practical attention to, what has come to be understood as food sovereignty.

The next section comprises short case studies on women, peace and security from different angles, and written by both activists and academics from Zimbabwe, Nigeria, Madagascar and the Democratic Republic of Congo (DRC). Netsai Mushonga gives us a general overview of the nexus between gender and security sector reform in Zimbabwe. Tosin Akinjobi-Babatunde looks back at the introduction of women into the Nigerian Police Force (NPF), and explores how patriarchy and limited notions of gender have constrained women's roles, operations and activities in the NPF ever since. Gaby Razafindrakoto highlights the challenges facing women and their inclusion in security sector reform processes in Madagascar. She draws our attention to the recent AU security sector reform needs assessment reports and the development of a UNSCR 1325 NAP that is in progress. Yolanda Sadie traces the slow progress made in the DRC towards addressing the overwhelming problem of sexual and gender-based violence (SGBV), despite numerous international commitments and national strategies. Sadie argues that unless and until the underlying gender norms and unequal power relations that form the basis of gender violence, discrimination and inequality in Congolese society are addressed, SGBV will persist.

The issue concludes with the Africa Watch section, wherein Hawa Mohammed explores the constitutional gains made for women in Kenya and Somalia over the last decade, as well as the challenges to gender equality that persist despite formal and legal progress.

Notes

1 United Nations, Beijing Declaration and Platform for Action, 1995, www.un.org/womenwatch/daw/beijing/pdf/BDPfA%20E.pdf (accessed September 2015).

2 SADC Protocol on Gender and Development, 2008, Johannesburg: Southern African Development Community.

Women, peace and security in Africa

Conceptual and implementation challenges and shifts

Cheryl Hendricks

This article highlights and critiques the underlying conceptualisations and assumptions of the women, peace and security (WPS) agenda that emerged with the adoption of United Nations Security Council Resolution 1325 in 2000. The main argument is that we need to rethink the WPS agenda to produce more holistic and groundbreaking responses for the types of challenges encountered, i.e., that gender inequality and insecurity are deep rooted and multi-layered, and thus negate mechanistic responses that do not deal with cultural and structural issues. It specifically focuses on gender and peace-making and gender and peacekeeping to point to the pitfalls in the current conceptions and practices in this arena.

Introduction

The year 2015 is a milepost for assessing progress and challenges in the quest for gender equality and for creating a more gender-sensitive and gender-responsive security sector globally. It is 20 years since the adoption of the Beijing Declaration and Platform for Action (1995), 15 years since the adoption of the United Nations Security Council Resolution (UNSCR) 1325 (2000), and it is the year in which the targets of the Millennium Development Goals (2000) and the Southern African Development Community (SADC) Protocol on Gender and Development (2008) should be met. Consequently, there has been a hive of activity geared towards gender 'stock-taking' and the setting of new goals and targets. In relation to peace and security, the United Nations (UN) conducted a high-level review and global study on women, peace and security and high-level reviews of the peacebuilding architecture and peacekeeping operations in 2015. These reviews are likely to play an important role in reconceptualising peacekeeping and peace-building and in shaping the future areas of engagement on women, peace and security (WPS).

The African Union (AU) is a leading organisation for setting the normative agenda on gender equality on the continent. It is active in advocating for gender mainstreaming, in accordance with UNSCR 1325, in peace and security processes. The AU's Protocol to the African Charter on Human and Peoples' Rights on the Rights of Women (2003), Solemn Declaration of Gender Equality in Africa (2004), Gender Policy (2009), Framework for Post Conflict Reconstruction and Development (2006), and Policy Framework for Security Sector Reform (2011) all call for gender equality and women's inclusion in peace and security structures and processes.[1] Under the current stewardship of Nkosazana Dlamini-Zuma, appointed as Chairperson of the AU Commission in 2012, there is a more concerted effort by the AU on mainstreaming gender into peace and security. For example, the AU appointed Bineta Diop as Special Envoy on WPS, launched a five-year gender, peace and security programme, is developing a 'Continental Results Framework' for women, peace and security,[2] and has themed the Heads of State Summits for 2015 around women's empowerment.

Global and continental efforts at gender mainstreaming in peace and security have been accompanied by state-level attempts to increase the participation of women in their security sector, as well as in peacekeeping deployments, and by civil society activism across the continent advocating for the implementation of UNSCR 1325.

Despite all the frameworks, agenda setting, national action plans, advocacy and training, however, 15 years post UNSCR 1325 there is little substantive progress in increasing women's participation in peace and security structures and processes and in creating greater security for women. In 2004, the UN Secretary General called for member states to adopt national action plans (NAPs) to ensure implementation of the resolution. Currently, only 50 countries (out of 196) have these plans, 15 (30%) of which are in Africa, and very few of these are actually being realised.[3] Women remain marginal to peace processes, with less than 4% as signatories to peace agreements and less than 10% as negotiators at peace tables.[4] The UN has made little progress in the deployment of women peacekeepers, performing below the envisaged targets of 10% for military and 20% for police (women only constitute 3% of the military and 10% of the police who are deployed on peace missions).[5] Data on gender representation in the national security sector institutions in Africa remains largely inaccessible.

Significantly, there has been little visible translation of the drive for women's participation in the security sector into actual security for women. Sexual and gender-based violence (SGBV) in conflict areas remains high, and accusations of peacekeepers abusing women and children abound, blurring the boundaries between perpetrators and protectors. Moreover, violence against women is not confined to conflict situations; it is arguably more pervasive, and part of the 'everyday' experiences of women in countries not considered to be involved in conflict. SGBV is also not limited to the public sphere – domestic violence is as ubiquitous, and it is the bane of women, girls, boys and, to a lesser extent, men. Beyond physical violence, women's security in many countries is constrained by 'structural violence'[6] – access to food, water, shelter, sanitation, employment, health care, discriminatory and exclusionary cultures, and so forth – creating general conditions of human insecurity. Post 9/11 we have also seen the remilitarisation of our societies, the normalisation of violence and the re-ascendance of a hyper-masculinity, all of which reinforce patriarchy and undermine the agenda of creating gender equality and peace and security for women. Therefore, there is a need to extend the focus and implementation of UNSCR 1325 beyond its predominant conflict–country application, and we must have a far broader view of the sources of insecurity for women.

After decades of feminist theorising, gender activism and the collation of empirical data, we know much more about the interrelationship between gender and security, and the security challenges facing women, especially in Africa. This accumulation of knowledge has been the drive behind the frameworks and programmes that have been adopted and implemented, but the application has had less than the desired impact for gender transformation within the security sector. Much of the explanation to date has been on the implementation gap, hence the call for better measuring tools and accountability mechanisms. Though this may be necessary, it is a rather depoliticised, technical response to issues that are fundamentally about reconstructing gender power relations.

This article, and others in this special issue of *African Security Review*, highlights the need for a different set of questions that may assist in moving the WPS agenda out of the cul-de-sac it appears to be trapped in; i.e., more and more resolutions and programming, but little headway in terms of increasing women's participation, transforming institutions and cultures, and improving the security of women. These questions relate to determining the dominant conceptualisation of the WPS agenda. Where are the conceptual limitations in the discourse? What explains the gaps between theory, policy and practice? What are the new conversations transpiring around issues of gender and security in Africa, and how should these inform an agenda moving forward? What are the implementation challenges in relation to gender, peace and security in Africa?

This article provides a brief overview of the theoretical and advocacy interventions that created the space for the adoption of UNSCR 1325 in 2000, unpacks the conceptualisation of the WPS agenda, and, through the purview of what has become the doctrine for conflict management – peace-making, peacekeeping and peacebuilding – discerns the assumptions, challenges and progress of mainstreaming gender into the security sector. The main argument of this article is that we need to rethink the WPS agenda to produce more holistic and groundbreaking responses for the type of challenges encountered; i.e., that gender inequality and insecurity are deep rooted and multi-layered, and thus negate mechanistic responses that do not deal with cultural and structural issues. The majority of the interventions to date have not dealt with the key issues of patriarchy, militarism and 'gender normative violence' (e.g., routine coercion, domination, violence, and the silencing of women and girls),[7] and the 'vast majority of women, therefore, remain unequal, insecure and unsafe during both peace and war'.[8]

From theory to practice

The end of the Cold War opened the space for new critical thinking on peace and security, questioning the then taken for granted interpretations of how the world worked, how peace and security were to be attained, and whose knowledge and experiences counted. Old state-centric, status-quo-oriented, male-dominated Realist perspectives of security gave way to new conceptualisations, actors and issues that were broadly grouped into 'Critical Security Studies'. Feminist international relations and feminist security studies scholars and activists employed a gender lens for analysing war to determine where the women were and what was happening to them, and/or to highlight the gendered constructions and impact of war, and argued for recognition of the role of women as both victims and actors during conflict.[9] By the 1990s, security was being redefined from a narrow, national-interest interpretation to security as emancipation, as centred on individuals, as the ability to exercise choice and live in dignity, as linked to development, as situated in regional complexes, and as gendered. There was recognition of the roles of non-state actors and the broadening of security issues. These ideas, some of which coalesced into the human security approach, were advocated by the Aberystwyth, Copenhagen and Frankfurt schools and among feminist, post-colonial and post-modernist scholars. The ideas marked a fundamental rupture from the previously dominant conservative academic and policy discourses centred on national security.

The Nairobi Forward Looking Strategies (1985) highlighted that 'peace cannot be realised under conditions of economic and sexual inequality, denial of basic human rights and fundamental freedoms ... ', and it also made an explicit link between peace and development.[10] The Beijing Declaration (1995), a decade later, noted that 'local, national, regional and global peace is attainable and is inextricably linked to the advancement of women, who are a fundamental force for leadership, conflict resolution and the promotion of lasting peace at all levels'.[11] Moreover, one of its 12 themes specifically dealt with women in armed conflict; by that time the atrocities committed against women in the conflicts in Bosnia, Liberia, Sierra Leone, and so forth, had already gained the attention of world leaders. The Beijing Platform for Action advocated for gender mainstreaming as a strategy to advance gender equality and to ensure the development of gender-sensitive policies and programming.[12]

Five years later, in 2000, after much lobbying and a coalescing of interests of feminist scholars, gender activists and policymakers, UNSCR 1325 was unanimously adopted.[13] From the above, it is clear that while WPS issues were the subject of scholarly articles and UN frameworks prior to 2000, the adoption of UNSCR 1325 came to be seen as a 'founding moment for women peace and security'.[14] Its uniqueness is in its adoption by the highest international security body – the United Nations Security Council (UNSC), as opposed to the General Assembly – constituting the issue as one of security, to be dealt with in mainstream peace and security processes concerned with protection, prevention and participation, predominantly in peace support operations. The Secretary-General would also have to account on progress made on WPS on an annual basis. UNSCR 1325 has subsequently been augmented by resolutions 1820 (2008), 1888 (2009), 1889 (2009), 2106 (2013) and 2122 (2013), all of which seek to broaden and strengthen UNSCR 1325. This emerging WPS architecture, though not explicit, required national security institutions to become gender representative and gender responsive, and promote gender equality – and it necessitated that women's organisations become 'security literate' in order to effectively advocate for, and monitor, the implementation of the resolutions. It was therefore quickly integrated into security sector reform (SSR) programming in post-conflict countries. There are, however, many conceptual and practical challenges that spring from the implementation of the WPS agenda. Here I seek to highlight a few of the more general challenges, before proceeding to note the problems related to peace-making and peacekeeping in Africa.

The first important conceptual issue is the severing of the discourse and implementation of UNSCR 1325 from the broader feminist scholarship and activism on gender, peace and security that birthed it, and the consequent reduction of the focus on women. Feminists were concerned with how war and the institutions associated with it depended on specific constructions of masculinity and femininity, and how security institutions and militarisation created and entrenched hierarchical gender relations. Feminism was a 'political movement for women's rights and gender emancipation',[15] it was 'neither just about women, nor the addition of women to male stream constructions'.[16] However, in the translation from theory to practice, i.e., the institutionalisation of the WPS agenda through practices such as gender mainstreaming in the security sector, the agenda was narrowed to women's inclusion in peace and security processes and structures. There was little problematising of these processes or the security structures and their inherent gendered power relations. As Mathers noted, 'militaries do not only depend on women; they also depend on gender'.[17] Militaries are constructed as masculine spaces that require women to be at home, taking care of the reproductive costs.

There has also been little reflection on the differences between women in conflict and post-conflict environments: the uncovering of the different roles that women play in conflict and post-conflict situations that feminists had highlighted were soon displaced by a homogenised view of women as victims in need of protection. Indeed, countering SGBV became *the* rationale for women's inclusion into peacekeeping and/or the security sector and peace processes. Women's physical security therefore became prioritised to the exclusion of rights-based arguments and other security issues that had animated the human security debates (for example, social and economic security, dignity, access to health, etc.).[18] Gender became instrumentalised and treated as 'a policy input rather than a normative ideal based on equality as well as recognition of difference'.[19] In short, the transformative potential of applying a gendered lens to the security sector was blunted.

Gender mainstreaming was the adopted strategy through which a gender-sensitive and gender-responsive security sector would be created – similar to that of the development and political sectors and emerging from the Beijing Platform for Action. Although the UN definition of gender main-streaming is centred on 'assessing the implications for women and men of any planned action, including legislation, policies and programmes … with the ultimate goal to achieve gender equality', in practice this was skewed towards representation.[20] Sally Baden and Anne Marie Goetz, as early as 1997, reflected on the limitations of gender mainstreaming.[21] They noted that it focused on process and means rather than ends; that it became synonymous with women; that gender sensitivity was reduced to gender disaggregated data; that the relational aspects of gender, power and ideology and how patterns of subordination are reproduced were lost; and that there was a failure to recognise the gendered nature of the institutions themselves.[22] These limitations were replicated, a decade later, in the peace and security sector.

UNSCR 1325 provided the platform for mainstreaming gender into the security sector. It was a resolution essentially focused on peace missions, but was soon widely interpreted as one calling for women's participation in the security sector as a whole, and it was thus integrated into SSR pro-gramming, often as a 'soft entry' point for engaging in SSR in countries where this proved difficult (e.g., South Sudan, Zimbabwe). The DCAF/INSTRAW Geneva Centre for the Democratic Control of the Armed Forces UN International Research and Training Institute for the Advance-ment of Women toolkit on gender and SSR was the first comprehensive set of guidelines on how to mainstream gender into the various security sector institutions, and it was soon followed by a number of manuals and guidelines, including those produced by the UN.[23] These guidelines pre-faced the 'operational effectiveness' argument as the dominant reason for why women should be integrated into the security sector, often positing women with unique attributes that would make them better peacekeepers, negotiators, police officers, and so forth; i.e., essentialising women. They also inadvertently placed the burden of creating a more gender-responsive security sector on women's shoulders. This produced a situation in which women in the security sector now needed to rationalise and/or justify their presence in this sector.

Clarke argued that women's inclusion was fashioned in a way that 'treats them either as over-looked beneficiaries or as sources of knowledge and skills which will enhance the world of the security structures'.[24] Bendix highlighted that the discourse had de-thematised masculinity, despite dealing with institutions that are almost exclusively male dominated, and that it perpetuated a colonial framework of power relations (i.e., it cast non-Western women as victims and men as perpetrators of violence, and Western women as empowered and modern).[25] Clearly there was a divide setting in between practitioners and theorists, and this divide has widened over the last five years, with many African women theorists contesting the ways in which gender mainstreaming in the security sector is transpiring on the continent. Olonisakin highlighted that the security provisions for women had not changed:

> actors may have changed and spaces expanded for the inclusion of new actors but in reality the interests and frameworks that sustain the status quo remain entrenched ... security narratives transferred from extra-African sources do not bear much resemblance to the security needs of the vast majority of Africans, not least women.[26]

Hendricks and Olonisakin indicated that

> gender remains on the periphery, ghettoised in the peace and security architectures. There are, thus, two international peace and security agendas: the women, peace and security agenda and the peace and security agenda, with the latter not needing the prefix of men, but for all intents and purposes, protecting and projecting the needs and interests of men as universal. If we are to make headway, we need to break down these dichotomies and barriers so that we all work on, and toward, the same peace and security agenda.[27]

These conceptual flaws have impacted on the gender-transformation process in the security sector, largely limiting it to token participation in stereotypical gendered roles. The next section explores these conceptual and implementation flaws further by specifically analysing the integration of gender into peace-making and peacekeeping in Africa (drawing on my tracking of women in the security sector in southern Africa for the SADC Gender Protocol Barometer).

Gender and peace-making

There has been a concerted effort to push for women's representation in peace-making (negotiations and mediation). Peace negotiations are key decision-making arenas for societies in conflict; UNSCR 1325 calls for more participation of women in peace and security decision-making. Much of the literature tracking women's engagement in peace processes highlights that they have been engaged in peace efforts during conflict, but that this was at the informal/local level. When peace processes are formalised, usually with an outside mediator, women become excluded from the process. The argument has been that women should be included at these peace tables because these are important political sites in which the future governance of the country is being designed and its spoils shared. It is also here that disarmament, demobilisation and reintegration (DDR) and SSR processes are first negotiated. Women therefore need to be present to ensure representation in a future government and its associated decision-making institutions, and to ensure that their needs and interests are taken care of.

Ban Ki Moon stated that 'bringing women to the peace tables improves the quality of agreements reached, and increases the chances of successful implementation'.[28] De Alwis et al. note that 'a peace agreement is about more than cease-fires. It also lays the groundwork for how the post-colonial society will be structured once a political settlement is achieved'.[29] However, as indicated above, despite the effort, few women actually get to sit at these peace tables. This is because access to peace tables is largely determined by the control any one group has over its armed men (and therefore its capacity to do harm) in any given conflict, and it is mediated by experts, the majority of them men, who 'parachute' into war torn countries to 'fix' conflicts. This has resulted in a certain 'cowboy' attitude toward mediation with a concern to notch up successfully signed cease-fire agreements rather than a longer-term commitment toward establishing a sustainable peace.[30]

The challenge that emerges is that women are struggling to get into these spaces without a concomitant problematising of the space itself, and that their participation actually legitimises the elitist agreements that are forged. There is little rethinking of other ways in which peace and stability can be forged. Peace agreements do not in and of themselves lead to peace, as the relapses into conflict in many countries indicate. Some of the questions that need to be asked are: why should negotiations be configured in these ways? Who makes these decisions? Which women should be present at the negotiations, and to do what? What kind of training are women receiving to be mediators and/or observers or 'experts'? What other ways are there of delivering peace?

To date, much of the justification for women's inclusion has centred on an assumed innately peaceful nature and ability to get men to see reason, i.e. drawing on stereotypes of women as nurturers and mothers. Often, the rationale, too, is because women are victims of war. Very few stress women's roles as actors in the conflict (and it is in this role that many of the political parties and rebel groups have actually sent the few women representatives), and/or that women have interests and are not neutral bystanders in conflict.

Interestingly, Ellerby, examining peace agreements from 1990 to 2005, notes that most agreements, whether women participated or not, do mention women and/or make some provision for them.[31] She also highlights the importance of a woman's agenda, political space for women to participate and gender consciousness processes as key factors for enabling gender-sensitive peace agreements.[32]

The fact that the transition phase from conflict to post conflict presents the greatest opportunity to effect change in gender power relations had been highlighted by Meintjies et al. some time ago.[33] It is important for women to participate in peace processes, but we must not be limited by the current spaces (mediation), i.e. we must also seek to change the very nature of the peace process itself, for it is largely designed to settle disputes between men with the ability to do harm. We must also not use stereotypical discourses in order to justify inclusion. De Alwis et al. stated that 'women should participate in peace processes ... because they are themselves political subjects with rights. Women do not need to be better than, or more peaceful than men to exercise those rights'.[34]

Over the last 15 years in southern Africa, there have been mediation efforts in the Democratic Republic of Congo (DRC), Lesotho, Zimbabwe and Madagascar. South Africa has always been a model for women's inclusion in peace processes and has acted as a mediator in the above-mentioned conflicts. In South Africa, women got together across party lines and demanded 30% representation at the negotiations. They also developed the Women's Charter, outlining the key gender equality principles that guided much of what they proposed during the negotiations, and hence the gender-sensitive peace agreement and later constitution. They however did not insist upon this in the conflicts they mediated in southern Africa, nor in any of the other countries in the rest of Africa that they have been engaged in.

In the 2003 Sun City talks to bring about peace in the DRC, women constituted 5% of the signatories, none of the mediators and 12% (40 out of 340) of the negotiating parties. In Zimbabwe's mediation process in 2008, women constituted none of the signatories, and 16% (1 out of 6) of the negotiating parties. Two women were part of two separate negotiating teams from South Africa, namely Mojanku Gumbi and Lindiwe Zulu. It is unclear how many women were part of the negotiations in Madagascar, but the roadmap negotiated in 2011 was not gender sensitive. Women, however, made substantive gains in terms of representation in Madagascar's parliament, from 17.5% to 23%.[35]

It is clear that the imperative to include women in peace processes in SADC is not a high priority, despite the UN, AU and SADC noting the need for it. South Africa also does not have a policy on women's participation in peace-making. To date, then, rhetoric has not matched practice on this score.

Gender and peacekeeping

UNSCR 1325 specifically calls for more women as peacekeepers and for the protection of women during conflict. To give effect to this, the UN Department of Peacekeeping Operations produced a policy directive in 2010. The principles for this directive are inclusiveness (peacekeepers must consult with both men and women in post-conflict countries); non-discrimination (ensure policies and decisions that uphold the equal rights of women and girls); and gender balance and efficiency.[36] The UNSC tracks the implementation of UNSCR 1325 on an annual basis through a number of indicators. Some of these are listed below, for illustration:

- the extent to which UN peacekeeping and other special political missions include information on the violations of the human rights of women and girls;
- the number and type of actions taken by the UNSC in relation to UNSCR 1325;
- the percentage of reported cases of sexual exploitation and abuse allegedly perpetrated by uniformed and civilian peacekeepers and humanitarian workers that are acted upon out of the total number of referred cases;
- the representation of women among mediators, negotiators, and technical experts in formal negotiations;
- the percentage of peace agreements with specific provisions to improve the security and status of women and girls; and
- the percentage of missions with senior gender advisors.[37]

The above is instructive of the bean counting that takes place on an annual basis without necessarily leading to an improvement in the protection of women and/or the deployment of more women peacekeepers. There is little in the list of indicators that actually measures impact.

The continued incidences of peacekeepers and humanitarian officials participating in the sex economy that develops around peace missions, despite codes of conduct and zero-tolerance policies, is a telling sign of the misguided notions of who protects whom from what. Everyone in these conflict spaces occupies multiple identities simultaneously: identities such as protector, victim, actor, perpetrator, buyer, seller, rebel, soldier, child, man, peacemaker, warmonger – it is a messy environment. The assumption that entry by women peacekeepers will somehow mitigate these tensions and that they would be able to reduce incidences of SGBV – by virtue of being women – is misplaced. They are not trained to do so nor do they have any better insight than their male counterparts into the gender dynamics of the countries they are being deployed to.

Baaz and Stern, in a seminal article, pointed out that soldiers rape because they have the opportunity to do so and because it is part of military and war culture.[38] We therefore need a much more nuanced analysis of conflicts and the gender dynamics within it – rather than the now universalised response of 'rape as weapon of war' and of SGBV as the automatic lens through which gender relations are unpacked. How do we factor in militarism, violent masculinities, and the political economies of gender and sexuality into our analysis? These have largely been omitted and hence the response mechanisms are often reactive (victim friendly units, mobile courts, etc.), when what is required is a fundamental rethink of peacekeeping and the cultures of the security sector institutions upon which peacekeeping depends, as well as a different discourse about gender relations within conflict contexts.

We should have women peacekeepers, not because they can necessarily change this situation but because those who want to go and perform this duty should have the right to do so, period – no other justification is needed! For change within the gender dynamics of peacekeeping to occur, we require a more system-wide structural and ideological emphasis, not simply more and different types of bodies. The call for more female-only peacekeeping units seems to be equally misplaced – it draws on constructs of women as 'natural bridge builders' and other essentialised and instrumentalised notions of women and the roles they can and should play. Lindy Heinecken has also echoed the call for female contingents, noting the need for an

> elite special forces women's Peace Corps [which has the] right gender mix for the right tasks, ranging from peacebuilding to peace enforcement. In addition to being capable infantry soldiers, the women in such a special corps should be specifically trained, equipped, and deployed to engage with women at the local community level and understand the local gender dynamics …. This kind of approach could not only enhance the capacity of female peacekeepers, but could also empower local women in countries affected by armed conflict by providing an important link in addressing their specific needs and assisting them in their attempts to bring about a sustainable peace.[39]

This begs the question of why it is not possible to train all peacekeepers to do this. In fact the problem is not male or female peacekeepers that will provide better protection for, and engage more with, women and the local populace; the problem is inherent in the institution of peacekeeping itself. The fact that we are increasingly moving towards peace enforcement also does not bode well for the deployment of female peacekeepers who are seen as a liability in these contexts, and hence the drop in the numbers of females deployed to them.

In southern Africa, we do well in terms of the number of women we deploy as peacekeepers. This is directly related to the relatively high number of women that are in the security sector – a legacy of women's participation in the liberation struggles of the region.

Table 1 and Figure 1 below highlight the levels of representation of women in the defence forces in SADC and the ratio of women to men being deployed from the respective countries in the region as peacekeepers. South Africa is well known for the high levels of representation of women in the security sector. As indicated below, in 2015 it reached the 30% mark for women in the defence forces (it similarly has high levels of women in the police force, e.g., 34%). It also deploys, in absolute numbers, the largest number of women peacekeepers in the region – but in terms of percentage of male to female, Zimbabwe and Namibia have a better balance. However, the number of women in the security sector says nothing about the levels of security of women in South Africa. Here, we see some of the highest levels of SGBV and female homicides. For example, in the 2013–4 period, for which crime statistics were collated by the South African Police Service, 17 068 people (which includes 2 354 women) were murdered (five times higher than the global average), while 46 245 people were raped and 62 649 people sexually assaulted.[40] Similarly, for peacekeeping, the number of women in a contingent says very little about the level of security provided to women in conflict areas. Preventing SGBV and affording women protection requires a much more holistic, integrated and targeted response than those seen to date, either in conflict or post-conflict areas.

Table 1 Percentage of women in the SADC's defence forces in 2015

Country	Male	Female
South Africa	70%	30%
Namibia	77%	23%
Zimbabwe	80%	20%
Seychelles	80%	20%
Lesotho	90%	10%
Zambia	90%	10%
The DRC	97%	3%
Malawi	92%	8%
Mozambique	95%	5%
Botswana	99%	1%
Madagascar	99%	1%
Tanzania	No data	
Swaziland	No data	
Angola	No data	

Source: Statistics compiled by C Hendricks, Conflict resolution and peacebuilding, in Sifiso Dube and Lucia Makamure (eds), *SADC Gender Protocol Barometer*, Johannesburg: GenderLinks, 2015.

Figure 1   Percentage of women deployed by SADC countries 2013–4

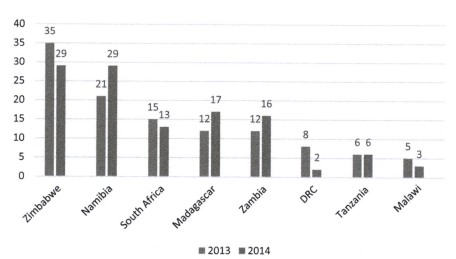

Source: Statistics compiled by C Hendricks, Conflict resolution and peacebuilding, in C Lowe-Morna Sifiso Dube, Lucia Makamure (eds) (ed.), *SADC Gender Protocol Barometer*, Johannesburg: GenderLinks, 2015.

Conclusion

To conclude, the struggle for gender equality has provided the necessary frameworks for women to assert their rights to representation, participation, protection and empowerment, and to live with dignity. Translating these gains into the lived realities for most women, but especially for those in conflict areas, has been challenging. UNSCR 1325 and subsequent WPS resolutions provide a framework to mobilise for more gender-representative and gender-responsive peace processes. However, its application to date has been seriously limited and limiting. This article has argued that these limitations emerge because of the ways in which the WPS agenda has been reconstructed away from its previous potential to bring radical reform to security sector institutions and peace and security discourses and practices. Instead, it has become managerial, technocratic and overly concerned with numbers, thereby ignoring vested power relations. This then has entrenched patriarchal attitudes and violent masculinity in the sector, rather than bringing about the envisaged gender equality or increased security for women. We therefore must have a review of the very processes and institutions themselves, and not merely seek to be included, which merely serves to validate structures and processes not designed to further the collective interest of all citizens. In short, there needs to be a conceptual shift from women to gender, from inclusion to transformation, and from numbers to impact. The call is for more nuanced, more integrated and more reflective approaches to the peace and security agenda at large, and to gender peace and security in particular.

Notes

1 African Union, Protocol to the African Charter on Human and Peoples' Rights on the Rights of Women in Africa. Adopted by the AU on 11 July 2003. African Union, Solemn Declaration on Gender Equality in Africa adopted by the AU in July 2004. African Union, African Union Gender Policy. Adopted by the AU in 2009 African Union, African Union Policy on Post-Conflict Reconstruction and Development (PCRD), adopted in Banjul in 2006. African Union Commission, African Union Policy Framework on Security Sector Reform, adopted in Addis Ababa in 2011.

2 UN Women, Recommendations towards a continental results framework on women, peace and security in Africa, March 2015, www.un.org/en/africa/osaa/pdf/events/20150310/report.pdf, (accessed August 2015).

3 Institute for Inclusive Security, The Power of a Plan, https://actionplans.inclusivesecurity.org/, (accessed 5 October 2015).

4 UN Women, Facts and figures: peace and security, www.unwomen.org/en/what-we-do/peace-and-security/facts-and-figures, (accessed August 2015).

5 UN, Report of the Secretary-General on women, peace and security, September 2013, S/2013/525, www.un.org/en/ga/search/view_doc.asp?symbol=S/2013/525, (accessed August 2015).

6 To employ a concept coined by Johan Galtung, Violence, Peace and Peace Research, *Journal of Peace Research*, 6: 3, 1969, pp 167–191.

7 A concept employed by Margaret Walker, cited in D Mazurana and K Proctor, Gender, conflict and peace, World Peace Foundation Occasional Paper, October 2013, http://fletcher.tufts.edu/~/media/Fletcher/Microsites/World%20Peace%20Foundation/Gender%20Conflict%20and%20Peace.pdf, (accessed August 2015).

8 C Hendricks and 'F Olonisakin, Gender, peace and security: conceptual links to address persistent gender based violence and gender inequalities in conflict and post conflict situations, unpublished paper produced for the African Development Bank's High Level Panel on Fragile States, 2014, 2.

9 For example, see C Enloe, *Bananas, beaches and bases: making feminist sense of international politics*, Berkeley, CA: University of California Press, 1989; R Grant, The quagmire of gender and international security, in VS Peterson (ed.), *Gendered states: feminist (re)visions of international relations theory*, Boulder, CO: Lynne Rienner, 1992; VS Peterson, Transgressing boundaries: theories of knowledge, gender and international relations, *Millennium: Journal of International Studies*, 21, 1992. See also C Hendricks, *Gender and security in Africa: an overview*, Discussion Paper No. 63, Uppsala: Nordic Africa Institute, 2011.

10 UN, Nairobi Forward Looking Strategy for the Advancement of Women, adopted by the World Conference to review and appraise the achievements of UN Decade for Women: Equality, Development and Peace, Nairobi: UN, 1985, 13.

11 UN, Beijing Declaration, adopted at the Fourth World Conference for Women, Beijing: UN, 1995.

12 C Hendricks & 'F Olonisakin, Engaging (in)security as an entry point for seeking redress in gender inequality in Africa, *Africa Peace and Conflict Journal*, 6:1, 2013.

13 For an elaboration on the convergence, see 'F Olonisakin, C Hendricks, and A Okech, The convergence and divergence of three pillars of influence in gender and security, this issue.

14 L Sjoberg and JA Tickner, Introduction: international relations through feminist lenses, in JA Tickner and L Sjoberg (eds.), *Feminism and international relations: conversations about the past, present and future*, London: Routledge, 2011.

15 Ibid., 5.

16 Ibid., 5 (citing VS Peterson).

17 J Mathers, Women and state military forces, in C Cohn (ed.), *Women and wars*, Cambridge: Polity Press, 2013, 124.

18 J True, Feminist problems with international norms, in JA Tickner and L Sjoberg (eds.), *Feminism and international relations: conversations about the past, present and future*, London: Routledge, 2011.

19 Ibid., 81.

20 UN Women, Gender mainstreaming, extract of the report of the Economic and Social Council for 1997, www.un.org/womenwatch/daw/csw/GMS.PDF, (accessed August 2015).

21 S Baden and AM Goetz, Who needs (sex) when you can have (gender)? Conflicting discourses on gender at Beijing, *Feminist Review*, 56, 1997.

22 Ibid.

23 M Bastick and K Valasek (eds.), *Gender and security sector reform toolkit*, DCAF, OSCE/ODIHR, and UN Instraw, Geneva, 2008; UN SSR Taskforce, *Security sector reform, integrated technical guidance notes*, New York, 2012.

24 Y Clarke, Security sector reform in Africa: a lost opportunity to deconstruct militarized masculinities, *Feminist Africa*, 10, 2008, 59.

25 D Bendix, A review of gender and security sector reform: bringing the post-colonial and gender theory into the debate, in M Jacob, D Bendix, and R Stanley (eds.), *Engendering security sector reform*, Berlin: Free University of Berlin, 2008.

26 'F Olonisakin Evolving Narratives of Security Governance in Africa, in 'F Olonisakin and A Okech (eds), *Women and security governance in Africa*, Cape Town, Pambazuka press, 26.

27 C Hendricks and 'F Olonisakin, Gender, peace and security: conceptual links to address persistent gender based violence and gender inequalities in conflict and post conflict situations, unpublished paper produced for the African Development Bank's High Level Panel on Fragile States, 2014. See also C Hendricks & 'F Olonisakin, Engaging (in)security as an entry point for seeking redress in gender inequality in Africa, *Africa Peace and Conflict Journal*, 6:1, 2013.

28 Women must play full part in peace-building, Security Council declares, UN News Centre, 5 October 2009, www.un.org/apps/news/story.asp?NewsID=32424#.Veb5ICWqpBc

29 M De Alwis, J Mertes, and T Saijjad, Women and peace processes, in C Cohn (ed.), *Women and wars*, Cambridge: Polity Press, 2013, 171.

30 Ibid.

31 K Ellerby, (En)gendered security: the complexity of women's inclusion in peace processes, *International Interactions: Empirical and Theoretical Research in International Relations*, 39, 2013.

32 K Ellerby, *The tale of two Sudans: engendered security and peace processes*, Washington, DC: United States Institute for Peace, 2012.

33 S Meintjies, M Trushen, and A Pillay, *The aftermath: women in post-conflict transformation*, London: Zed Books, 2002.

34 M De Alwis, J Mertes, and T Saijjad, Women and peace processes, in C Cohn (ed.), *Women and wars*, Cambridge: Polity Press, 2013, 171.

35 C Hendricks, Conflict resolution and peacebuilding, in C Lowe-Morna, S Dube and L Makamure (eds), *SADC Gender Protocol Barometer*, Johannesburg: GenderLinks, 2015.

36 UN DPKO, Policy: gender equality in peacekeeping operations, 2010, www.un.org/en/peacekeeping/documents/gender_directive_2010.pdf, (accessed August 2015).

37 UN, Report of the Secretary-General on women, peace and security, September 2013, S/2013/525, www.un.org/en/ga/search/view_doc.asp?symbol=S/2013/525, (accessed August 2015).

38 M Baaz & M Stern, Why do soldiers rape? Masculinity, violence and sexuality in the armed forces of the DRC, *International Studies Quarterly*, 53, 2009.

39 L Heinecken, Are female peacekeepers making a difference, and if not why not?, *Kujenga Amani*, 9 April 2015, http://forums.ssrc.org/kujenga-amani/2015/04/09/are-female-peacekeepers-making-a-difference-and-if-not-why-not/#.VegnMSWqpBc, (accessed September 2015).

40 Institute for Security Studies and Africa Check, Fact sheet: South Africa's official crime statistics 2013/2014, http://africacheck.org/factsheets/factsheet-south-africas-official-crime-statistics-for-201314/, (accessed June 2015).

The convergence and divergence of three pillars of influence in gender and security

'Funmi Olonisakin, Cheryl Hendricks and Awino Okech

This article explores the convergence between three pillars of influence – feminist security studies, civil society activism and policy decision-making – and its role in the adoption and implementation of United Nations Security Council Resolution (UNSCR) 1325. It argues that these three pillars, individually and collectively, have made important contributions to the debate and action on the gender and security agenda, but that they remain organically disconnected. Their convergence has the potential to achieve path-breaking results in the sphere of gender and security, whilst their divergence makes transformation unattainable. We show the disconnect in the application of UNSCR 1325 in Africa and argue that this is partly the reason why, despite enormous efforts, the gains realised in terms of gender equality in the peace and security arena have been negligible.

Introduction

Efforts to redress gender inequality remain confined to the periphery of the international security agenda, notwithstanding an evident increase in policy intervention and an active civil society, including academic engagement. Scholarly analysis has continued to offer insights into the drivers of gender inequality and its manifestations in the international security arena.[1] The adoption of policy frameworks such as United Nations Security Council Resolution (UNSCR) 1325 suggests that there is hope for a qualitative shift in the conditions that sustain gender inequality in regions like Africa, where two decades of armed conflict have created excessive inequalities. However, the absence of meaningful change for women in many corners of the continent after more than a decade of efforts to implement this change, and subsequent resolutions, raises fundamental questions about the relevance and quality of these interventions and actions.

While there have been many policy instruments and statements from regional and global policy actors alike intended to redress gender inequity,[2] the question remains as to whether peace- and security-related policy instruments can succeed in transforming gender inequality in Africa. The extent to which the arena of peace and security has drawn attention to gender inequality, but also delivered tangible outcomes, and the role of specific constituencies of actors in this process is the focus of this article. We explore the degree of coherence between the prominent narratives surrounding gender inequality and the approaches to addressing them. To what extent, for example, do the policy frameworks adopted in responding to gender inequality reflect feminist perspectives that propose a transformation in existing structures and power dynamics? Is the commitment and intention of those tasked with implementing these policies aligned with the agenda of gender equality? Or do they perform the role of guardian or gatekeepers to the structures that perpetrate gender inequality, which in turn sustains the cycles of insecurity for women?

This article identifies and discusses three pillars of influence on gender and security – feminist security analysis, civil society activism and policy decision-making. It argues that these three pillars, individually and collectively, have made important contributions to the debate and action on the gender and security agenda, but that they, notwithstanding their apparent interaction, remain organically disconnected.[3] We argue that their convergence has the potential to achieve path-breaking results while their divergence makes transformation unattainable. We illustrate this with the experiences that led to the adoption of UNSCR 1325 on women, peace and security, and subsequent efforts to implement this resolution in Africa. In this regard, we argue that despite evidence of significant efforts at the policy level, the gains realised in terms of gender equality in the peace and security arena in Africa are negligible.

Three pillars of influence and point of convergence

Three apparent pillars of influence have driven, in part, the gender and security agenda – globally and regionally. First is the analysis of feminists researching international relations and security studies, which highlights the gendered nature of security.[4] The second entails the activities of civil society organisations, including women's groups, which have demonstrated a measure of consistency in advocating for gender equality in the post-Cold War period. Typically, these organisations actively engage policy practitioners to promote gender-sensitive policies or their application where such policies are in existence. The third includes a cross-section of policy actors at global, regional and national levels, particularly those with the clout to influence or make policy decisions.

Individually, these pillars have made notable contributions to the gender and security discourse and practice. But their convergence offers the promise of transformation – conceptually and practically – of the terrain on which gender inequality thrives. A convergence of these pillars, for example, led to the adoption of UNSCR 1325, which was path-breaking at the time of its adoption in October 2000. UNSCR 1325 marked the first time that the issue of gender inequality and, in particular, the disproportionate impact of armed conflict on women and their gross under-representation in peace processes, had entered the agenda of the United Nations Security Council (UNSC).

Feminist security analysis

An examination of the trajectory of feminist security analysis reveals a relatively recent, piecemeal yet multi-layered engagement of feminist analysts with the subject of gender and security.

Traditional security and strategic studies were not concerned with the experience of individuals and as such it was difficult to highlight the gendered nature of security. Security discourse, particularly in the Cold War era, was state-centric – and understandably so. Analysis responded almost exclusively to the dominant events and narratives of that era. The prevailing realist paradigm concentrated attention on the state and its defence. The defence of the state was in turn viewed within the context of a bipolar world embroiled in a nuclear arms race and the restraining danger of superpower confrontation. Little or no attention was paid to events below the level of the state. As such, the security and safety of individuals had little room in security analysis, let alone any associated issues of gender inequality.

In effect, Africa and the experiences of ordinary Africans were peripheral to this consideration. African states emerged at the heart of the Cold War and inevitably constructed their security and politics to suit the demands of a bipolar world. Immediate post-independent and successive regimes, with very few exceptions, aligned themselves with either side of the Cold War divide. They either leaned toward Soviet-led communist ideology or the Western alliance capitalist stance, even though many of them retained membership of the Non-Aligned Movement. Indeed, while African history and politics were naturally at the core of teaching curriculums and research programmes, international relations (including its strategic studies branch) only emerged as a prominent field of study within African institutions and among African analysts during the 1980s.

The idea that security might be framed to include the personal experiences of individuals – one of the features of feminist theorising – featured little in security studies in Africa. The region had conclusively received a top-down, Anglo-American conception of security. In any case, conceiving of security in state-centric and militaristic ways was well suited to the agenda of regimes that had seized the advantage of a Cold War terrain to entrench themselves in power and adopt narratives that were attractive to their superpower allies. In that dispensation, the character of African states and, in particular, the internal conduct of regimes was far removed from the considerations of their great power allies. The plight of hundreds of millions of citizens who were excluded from access to resources or political participation was far from the radar of the leading powers. Not surprisingly, gender inequality, which was itself a key feature of the entrenched patriarchal structures in these states, was not about to leap to the fore of national and regional attention under those conditions.

To the extent that they engaged in security discourses, feminist analysts responded to the prevailing global security patterns. The role and structure of the institutions dedicated to the defence of the state and to the maintenance of the prevailing international security system provided an obvious channel of engagement.[5] Scholars such as Cynthia Enloe, V Spike Peterson and J Ann Tickner challenged the partial representations of war proffered by (neo-)realists, contending that they essentially denoted the experiences of men, and 'that International Relations assumptions were grounded in an increasingly unviable assertion of the state as the protector'.[6] In addition, the notion of 'alternative defence' articulated by Booth and Baylis,[7] among others, was initially peripheral to global security considerations. It, however, provided an avenue and the possibility of bringing to the fore security situations below the level of the state with individuals as a central focus. Hendricks noted:

> The work of feminist international relations scholars dovetailed with the general rethinking of security in the post-Cold War context. By 1989, the Soviet Union collapsed and with it the bipolar rivalry that dominated global security discourse for the preceding four decades. Traditional security paradigms were becoming irrelevant in explaining the apparent shift from interstate to intra-state conflicts. The new security paradigm therefore focused on broadening

the concept of security to include the referents of security (to the individual) and a widening of the range of actors involved in the provision of security.[8]

The outbreak of intra-state conflict was inevitable in Africa, particularly in the absence of the protection offered by superpower clients who courted and supported African governments on the basis of their ideological leanings. 'Rogue' states and leaders had maintained the facade of state-hood over the massive insecurities suffered by their people. Scholars and analysts no doubt began to respond to these events. As they did, alternative analyses, which did not gain visibility during the Cold War era and were previously overshadowed by military and strategic studies, began to gain ascendency.[9] Yet, as Hudson points out, analysis pursued by the 'Copenhagen school', epitomised by Buzan, still drew distinctions between social security where the security concerns of specific groups, such as women, were relegated and international security which dealt with 'collective' security concerns.[10] This distinction draws attention to the limited ways in which the structural factors that perpetuate gender inequality are understood, and therefore the limited ways in which the pathways to their resolution are defined.

One important school, which featured little in international security considerations during the Cold War, is that of peace studies. The work of Johan Galtung on structural violence and notions of positive and negative peace,[11] for example, has stood the test of time – but it was far removed from security considerations in strategic studies. Similarly, Kenneth Boulding's analysis of stable peace as an alternative to the unstable peace generated by strategic studies through notions of nuclear deterrence were peripheral to strategic studies and its umbrella discipline of international relations.[12] With the growing recognition of such seminal works, it became possible to think about peace and security as intertwined agendas – as two sides of the same coin. Perhaps even more significantly for security analysis, critical security theory emerged prominently, challenging the traditional notions of security and strategic studies. It moved away from the idea that the state is the central and perhaps only credible guarantor of security, and challenged realism's reduction of human nature and personal experiences.

Some of the more profound indications of a paradigm shift occurred in cases where analysts that were previously firmly associated with arguments about the correctness and/or supremacy of realist, state-centric thinking in security analysis acknowledged the solid contribution of feminist analysis. The link between theory and the self became acceptable, as opposed to strategic studies, which typically focus on the state and has little room for the perspectives of people: in the words of Booth, 'the personal, the political and the international are a seamless web'.[13]

Although feminist security analysis had already begun to assume a human security tone even before the concept was clearly articulated, it was the conduct of the largely intra-state armed conflicts in places like the former Yugoslavia and several parts of Africa that gave some prominence to feminist security analysis with specific focus on the gendered nature of insecurity not least the disproportionate impact on women.

The armed conflicts witnessed in Liberia (1989–1997) and later in Bosnia (1992–1995), Sierra Leone (1991–2002) and Somalia (1991–present) revealed the character of post-Cold War conflicts. The genocide in Rwanda (1994) was the most extreme manifestation of the conflicts. They were occurring within states, and warring parties freely committed gross atrocities against civilians. The very nature and conduct of these conflicts decidedly shifted attention and, invariably, the security debate to the terrain below the state. It was thus possible to discuss the security of individuals – and within this, that of particular groups of people. By 1994, the concept of human security had made its way to the top of the security discourse, albeit controversially. The notion that the individual ought to be the reference point in security is a central message of the human security concept, which gained ascendency from the first time it was elaborated upon in the *Human Development Report* published by the United Nations Development Programme (UNDP) in 1994.[14] The idea that individuals must achieve 'freedom from fear and freedom from want' in order to be secure became the central tenets of the human security discourse. The importance of seeing these two freedoms as not mutually exclusive is emphasised by scholars who argue that ensuring economic and social justice is as important as protecting people from violence.[15]

Feminist scholars were quick to point out the limited way in which gender was addressed in the human security discourse, noting that 'collapsing femininity or masculinity into the term "human" could conceal the gendered underpinnings of security practices'.[16] Lewis drew attention to the 'formulaic and ad hoc way' in which the human security discourse treated gender, and argued for the need to push the boundaries of the security discourse so that it could meaningfully deal with the insecurity in the domestic sphere.[17]

The subject of gender has not had as visible an impact on or dominated security analysis in the same way as ethnicity and religion, particularly within the context of intra-state conflict (with the exception of, and perhaps reduction to, a focus on rape). While gender may not always be the most important factor if taken as a unit of analysis in security discourse, it does, however, reveal an interconnected web of gendered practices across all levels.[18] The difficulty associated with gender is that it does not operate alone and interacts with other variables, which mutate at different moments. To manage difference requires resolving all other inequalities – to deal with one alone distorts the reality. The essence of this article's analysis of feminist scholarly engagement with the subject of security is not to explain the engagement, but to show how it influenced and evolved with the then new thinking in security studies.

There are two obvious points on which to rest the discussion of the trajectory of feminist security analysis in Africa. The first is the fact that a significant amount of feminist scholarly work on security is largely generated in the global North. Only a few African feminist scholars have taken this as a direct area of focus. Instead, what we see is a whole range of security analysis that is often rooted in the historical work of what women's movements have accomplished in terms of, for example, violence against women. African scholarship in this area is, however, increasingly stimulated by global militarisation and its impact on the continent and ongoing security sector reform initiatives. Africa's own attempt to offer feminist perspectives to African affairs has produced a small but growing collection of security analysis of direct relevance to Africa.[19]

However, in a continent that had been co-opted into a global security system in which the conduct of regimes and the well-being of the millions of excluded citizens were invisible in the global arena, feminist security analysis, despite its people-centred appeal, remained at a largely conceptual level. As such, while it had a high degree of appeal at least in the academic arena, translating it into robust policy agendas with extensive application did not occur. For any meaningful change to happen, it required that more feminist analysts engage the space of policy and activism. This is further discussed below.

Civil society activism

The second pillar of influence in gender and security consists of the activities of gender activists, women's groups and non-governmental organisations (NGOs) that have been instrumental in drawing attention to women's insecurity in particular contexts and facilitating relevant action. As will be shown later, the efforts of such activist groups predate the adoption of UNSCR 1325 and in fact facilitated its coming into being. We now look at the key factors that shaped the activism of this pillar of influence in favour of gender equality.

Campaigns and advocacy for gender equality in the peace and security arena has a pathway that compares with that of feminist security analysis, given that it has also been gradual and responsive to global events and processes. Certain milestones can be identified in the advocacy for gender equality across several decades. Four world conferences on women took place before 2000, in Mexico, Copenhagen, Nairobi and Beijing. It was in Beijing that a clear discussion took place about the insecurity faced by women in situations of armed conflict. Platform E, one of the 12 pillars in the outcome document of that conference, was devoted to the impact of armed conflict on women.

This focus on the impact of armed conflict occurred at the end of the Cold War, when the deadliness of the intra-state conflicts in Liberia, Sierra Leone, Bosnia and Rwanda had become apparent. The significant increase in atrocities against women in these and other armed conflicts produced the level of engagement seen among civil society actors on the issue of violence against women, globally. The advocacy of women's groups in the arena of peace and security grew by accretion, as wars in places like Bosnia and Rwanda wreaked maximum havoc and generated untold atrocities against women across generations.[20]

In the face of these difficult conflicts, efforts intensified in pursuit of the objectives outlined in the outcome document of the 4th World Conference on Women in Beijing in 1995, *Platform for Action*.[21] Annual forums such as the Committee on the Status of Women (CSW) became a convening point for strategising on the issues of women affected by armed conflict. It was in one such annual convening of the NGO Caucus on Women and Armed Conflict at the CSW that the idea of placing the issue of women in peace and security processes on the agenda of the UNSC was mooted.[22] By 1999, there was increased momentum, as a group of NGOs led by International Alert led a global campaign on 'Women Building Peace: From Village Council to the Negotiating Table'. Supported by some United Nations (UN) agencies such as the United Nations Development Fund for Women (UNIFEM), this civil society coalition pushed for the UNSC to take up this agenda. The Windhoek Declaration and Namibia Plan of Action of May 2000 maintained this momentum. It underscored the need to include gender dimensions in peace support operations – not least, training, leadership and mission structure.[23]

Women's organisations working in this arena have also been central to supporting peace initiatives where these have emerged. Notable here are the Somali Sixth Clan, Burundi women's contribution to the Arusha talks, Femmes Africa Solidarite (FAS), the Mano River Women's Peace Network (MARWOPNET), Women as Partners for Peace in Africa (WOPPA), the West African Peace Network (WANEP), South African Women in Dialogue (SAWID), and individual women such as Uganda's Betty Bigombe's contributions as a mediator in the protracted talks with the Lords Resistance Army's Joseph Kony. These are just some of the forums through which women's initiatives in mainstream conflict resolution efforts have surfaced.[24] More importantly, women's rights organisations have continually engaged institutions relevant to the maintenance of just peace such as the police and the judiciary through training and advocacy initiatives aimed at reforming institutional approaches to dealing with women-specific issues.

Policy decision makers and point of convergence

The third and last pillar of influence includes the action of policy decision makers. Their actions invariably close the intervention cycle in the effort to address the challenge of gender inequality in peace and security processes. The policy decisions made by this group of actors make it possible to pave the way toward change. The interdependence of thinking/ideas, policy analysis and action cannot be overstated. The policy aftermath of this interaction is clear evidence of the convergence of these pillars.

Africa, as the continent with the majority of conflict and post-conflict countries, has been a recipient of this combination of efforts, albeit in varying degrees. The second and third pillars of influence in particular have been adapted in various forms in Africa. The African Union (AU), regional economic communities and their respective member states, think tanks, NGOs and women at the community level are engaged with advocating and adopting strategies for gender mainstreaming in peace and security mechanisms.

Africa has been at the receiving end of global policy approaches and peacebuilding interventions for the past two decades. Indeed this could not but be the case given the scale of humanitarian tragedy that began to unfold when a number of African conflicts erupted into violence. These conflict situations challenged global and African institutions alike. In Africa, the Economic Community of West African States (ECOWAS) – a regional organisation founded for reasons of economic integration – was the first to break from the straitjacket of normative frameworks such as 'non-intervention in the internal affairs of member states' when it intervened on humanitarian grounds in the Liberian armed conflict. The UN and the Organisation of African Unity (OAU), the AU's predecessor, remained limited by their adherence to this norm for a few years. ECOWAS would later find itself intervening in the conflicts in Sierra Leone, Guinea Bissau and Cote d'Ivoire.

Before long, the agenda of the UN was occupied in large part by a string of African conflicts, although it was also dealing with conflict in other parts of the world, not least the former Yugoslavia and East Timor. Former UN Secretary-General Boutros Boutros-Ghali's *Agenda for Peace* and its supplement, *Another Agenda for Peace*, opened the path for expanded frameworks and approaches to peace-making and peacekeeping. This included, among other things, the notions of peacebuilding and post-conflict reconstruction, which were accommodated within multi-dimensional peacekeeping and peace support operations. In due course, the UN would come to deploy peacekeeping and/or observer missions in Somalia, Liberia, Sierra Leone and Rwanda, with varying degrees of effectiveness.

In the period since 2000 we have seen some of the manifestations of sustained action, whether in the form of new policy frameworks or the creation of new entities and institutions to champion the agenda of women in peace and security processes. This was the case when, in October 2000, the issue of women and armed conflict made it onto the agenda of the UNSC with the adoption of UNSCR 1325.

The coalition of civil society (including scholars) and policy actors that worked together to facilitate the adoption of UNSCR 1325 is striking evidence of what can happen when these pillars of influence converge. This was the case, for example, with the governments and ambassadors of Bangladesh, Jamaica, Canada, the Netherlands and the UK, who put their weights behind civil society organisations to champion the cause of women in peace and security processes at the UN in 2000.[25] This was a key action leading to the adoption of UNSCR 1325 in October 2000; it was clearly the result of the convergence of the analytical work of feminists, the activism of civil society and the weight of policy actors.

UNSCR 1325 and the pathway to application

The adoption of UNSCR 1325 drew international attention to the linkage between gender and security and the need to include women in the processes of peace-making, peacekeeping and peacebuilding. The resolution focuses on a number of issues around the impact of armed conflict on women and their role in conflict management and resolution processes. A core message that runs through the resolution is the need to integrate a gender perspective into peacebuilding and post-conflict reconstruction. The provisions of UNSCR 1325 are typically summed up as 'the 3Ps' – the *protection* of women, the *prevention* of armed conflict and the increased *participation* of women.

Overall, UNSCR 1325 is better conceived of in practical ways – and it is by no means a panacea to the challenges faced by women in peace and security processes. It is the result of a negotiated process – a compromise document that had to find common ground for all signatory states, and not just the states that were enthusiastic about promoting the women, peace and security agenda. As such, it could not meet the expectation that it would go deep enough to address the gender inequalities that are deeply embedded in the discourses surrounding international security institutions and processes, as highlighted by academics and analysts.[26]

Indeed, the compromising nature of UNSCR 1325 might account in part for the thinness of its application on the ground, as discussed below – but it is difficult to draw this conclusion from the patchy data that exists at the moment. On the surface, these three pillars present a picture of a concerted and effective response to the issue of gender inequality. A closer examination, however, reveals that the linkage between them is neither systematic nor deep. Mainstream security discourse, including debates on international security whether at global or regional level, rarely take on board feminist security analysis. Feminist perspectives on gender and security are invariably lost along the way and fail to gain depth in policy approaches and responses. There is no clarity as yet as to where and how the disconnect occurs.

What is apparent, however, is that the policy frameworks developed in response to gender inequality are easily removed from the centre stage of global security concerns. In the same vein, gender activists are easily relegated to the periphery of global and international security considerations, with an emphasis on the humanitarian nature of the challenges facing women, for instance. Gender-related security concerns are only tangentially connected to programmatic interventions designed to implement supposedly new radical international security agendas. Even in the few, typical exceptions such as peace processes, the 'add-on' nature of gender considerations and the superficial inclusion of women remain a regular feature. Similarly, gender concerns are simply added to mainstream security programmatic interventions, as seen, for example, in the areas of security and justice sector reform, post-conflict reconstruction and development.

The value of UNSCR 1325 in exploring this disconnectedness between policy and application is that it offers a prism through which one can view the pathway from analysis to decision-making and practical application. It might then be possible, over time, to systematically investigate this trajectory in order to understand the facilitators and disablers of transformation along this pathway. For now, what is clear is that the obvious convergence of feminist analysis, civil society activism and action by policy decision makers which led to the adoption of UNSCR 1325 has not been a tangible and consistent feature in its application in Africa. The efforts to apply UNSCR 1325 in Africa reveal little or no convergence between these pillars of influence.

The absence of qualitative change

Efforts to implement UNSCR 1325 are visible at several levels in the region. The first includes UN peace operations in Africa, which often serve as the channel for implementation of UNSCR 1325 in conflict-affected countries. The logic of the intervening role of peace operations and by extension the UN Department of Peacekeeping Operations (DPKO) in addressing gender inequality is easy to understand. As the leading actor for the restoration of peace in the conflict-affected states, it is the local society's first point of contact with universal norms, principles and policies in the peace implementation process. It is thus the actor best suited to begin the implementation of UNSCR 1325 in those settings. It can do so in a number of ways, including:

- Serving as a model by making its own internal framework and practices reflect the principles of UNSCR 1325;
- Reflecting gender perspectives throughout its programme design and implementation; and
- Reaching out to influence communities and systems in the countries where the UN peace mission is present through its mechanisms and staff, in particular through its gender offices.

Typically, the mandates of peace operations that came into being after the adoption of UNSCR 1325 are now explicit about the implementation of the provisions of the resolution, and UN operations have consistently included gender elements in their periodic reporting.[27]

It is tempting to be self-congratulatory about the attempts to implement UNSCR 1325 within UN operations. Ideally, the concern and attention of policymakers and practitioners as well as a readily interested and energised women's movement should by now be directed to one issue: how best to achieve similar results in the terrains where such peace operations are not present. But thus far, anecdotal evidence suggests that all of the above remain an aspiration rather than a reality. At present there are less than 10 post-conflict environments in Africa where the UN has a peacekeeping presence and where the weight of its institutions and policies can be brought to bear. In those settings, there is no real evidence that gender relations are being transformed or that gender equality is becoming a living reality.[28]

Serious gaps remain in the application of UNSCR 1325 by peace operations. Indeed, peace operations have become a microcosm of the deeper structural issues that serve as obstacles to the achievement of gender equality. The attitudes and values exhibited by many peace operations staff – who do not necessarily believe in or ascribe to gender equality – are part of the problem. As such, many are content to do no more than take a technical approach in dealing with this issue.[29] This factor appears to be one of the main disablers that prevent transformation in the translation of policies such as UNSCR 1325 into meaningful change in affected societies. Invariably, only the individual Gender Adviser or peace operation staff member with a genuine commitment to the issue of gender equality takes the extra step to go beyond merely 'ticking the box' in implementing gender-related policies.

We must hasten to add that while being potentially the first point of visible and organised UN contact with the organised parts of conflict-affected states and societies, actors connected to the UN DPKO and peace missions are often not the only UN presence on the ground. Apart from their contributions to multi-dimensional peace operations, other UN agencies – including UN Women (formerly UNIFEM), the UNDP, the Food and Agriculture Organisation, the World Food Programme and the United Nations Population Fund (UNFPA) – are often present in conflict-affected societies. While these agencies may interact with local communities in their respective areas of work expertise, opportunities always exist to reflect gender perspectives in their work in conflict-affected areas – and many of them often do. Indeed, agencies like the UNFPA and the UNDP, who are not directly tasked with the application of UNSCR 1325, have taken steps to implement UNSCR 1325-related programmes in a number of post-conflict contexts. As earlier indicated, the real challenge lies in the depth and concreteness of the application.

The application of UNSCR 1325 and related agenda by African regional organisations

The degree to which UNSCR 1325 has been embraced by African states and regional organisations can be reflected in the state of application of regional instruments and of national action plans. In areas without a significant UN presence, which applies to much of Africa, altering the policy and practice of regional actors offers a reasonable chance to influence the performance of its state members. The African Peace and Security Architecture (APSA) presents an ideal framework for implementing UNSCR 1325 and building an overall gender perspective in the work of the African Union Commission (AUC) and in the policies ratified by member states. Given that the Regional Economic Communities (RECs) form one of the 'building blocks' of APSA, implementing UNSCR 1325 and related policy frameworks in the RECs is vitally important for transmitting the values and principles of the resolution.

At the level of the AU, perhaps the most visible manifestation of the internalisation of UNSCR 1325 is the 'Solemn Declaration on Gender Equality in Africa' (SDGEA) of 2004.[30] This declaration explicitly mentions UNSCR 1325 and confirms the AU's commitment to some issues relating to women, peace and security, including gender-based violence and gender mainstreaming in peace processes. This instrument's articulation of the AU's commitment to the empowerment of women at the highest political levels will need to be matched by a willingness and ability to apply and systematise these principles into the daily life of the organisation.

A number of RECs have also taken steps to address gender-related security issues. Two RECs stand out in this regard – ECOWAS and the Southern African Development Community (SADC). ECOWAS is seeking to address gender and security issues through several platforms, such as the ECOWAS Conflict Prevention Framework (ECPF), which devotes a component to 'women, peace and security', and the development of a Plan of Action for this component. The Directorate of Human Development and Gender is now in the process of implementing this Plan of Action over a three-year period from 2013–2016.[31] SADC too has taken important steps toward addressing women, peace and security issues, including the SADC Protocol on Gender and Development of 2008, in which Article 28 calls for the implementation of UNSCR 1325, and the SADC gender policy which calls for the eradication of sexual and gender-based violence and all other forms of violence towards women and girls. These instruments have provided opportunities for SADC and its member states to apply the principles of UNSCR 1325.

Notwithstanding these developments at the level of the AU, and within RECs such as ECOWAS and SADC, there is still much to be done within these organisations. For example, women are far from the 50% mark for representation within the peace and security institutions and programmes of these organisations. The AUC has achieved better results in the appointment of women into senior leadership positions at the level of commissioner and directors, where there is near gender parity, but the organs and associated institutions have not fared as well as the top decision-making structures of the AU – the Heads of State Summit remains an overwhelmingly male sphere.[32] The AU has now also appointed Bineta Diop as the Special Envoy on Women Peace and Security and deploys gender advisors to its missions. However, just as the AU has been reluctant to shift to multi-dimensional peacekeeping, so too has there been no systematic shift in its approach to gender mainstreaming in its peace and security endeavours. Only time will tell whether the presence of the few formidable women now at the AU will be sufficient to create the necessary behavioural shift at the AU and its associated peace and security organs.

There have been a few AU peacekeeping and political missions in, for example, Burundi, Comoros, Sudan and Somalia. The AU Mission in Somalia (AMISOM) marks the first time there was a visible incorporation of gender considerations into an AU operation through the establishment of the position of a Gender Officer. The role of this officer is to ensure 'that matters of gender are mainstreamed in AMISOM policies and to follow up with the Somalia authorities and other actors to ensure gender mainstreaming in key policy decisions and undertakings'.[33] This was replicated in the African Mission in Mali (AFISMA), but there has been little analysis of the impact of these efforts.

In southern Africa, with its history of liberation struggles, women's participation in the security sector predate UNSCR 1325. The region showed promise that it might lead the way in the achievement of gender equality and provide lessons for the rest of the continent. However, though it has done relatively well in terms of women's representation, the security institutions have not sufficiently grappled with the thorny issues of whose security matters, how it should be provided and what needs to be done differently to ensure greater levels of security for all. That is, the gendered nature of norms, culture and security practices are seldom under scrutiny: UNSCR 1325 was never intended to engage that debate.[34]

Application of UNSCR 1325 at the national level

The effort to apply UNSCR 1325 transcends UN DPKO, UN agencies and regional institutions. By 2004, proposals for implementing UNSCR 1325 were being put forward. For example, in his report to the UNSC in 2004 on the agenda of women, peace and security, the UN Secretary-General proposed that member states take steps to implement UNSCR 1325 at the national level.[35] Gradually, the development of National Action Plans (NAPs) on UNSCR 1325 became a regular part of the agenda of a number of member states. National-level implementation has tended to focus on three areas: the participation of women in peace and security decision-making processes, the protection of women and girls, and gender training.

Currently 50 countries have approved NAPs on women, peace and security, 15 of which are African countries. It is instructive that African countries with approved NAPs are predominantly those that have experienced significant armed conflict in all or parts of their states.

While 'twinning' with donor country teams may have facilitated the war-affected countries' development of NAPs, the processes of developing these plans in the African countries concerned have been, by and large, 'inclusive' and have looked at women, peace and security issues in a 'holistic' way.[36] Post-conflict contexts in which peacebuilding is actively undertaken still remain the best opportunity to include gender issues in ways that are not possible in countries that have not experienced open armed conflict.

However, even with these few African countries with NAPs, it is difficult to observe real transformation in the key areas that form the focus of NAPs. Perhaps one exception is Rwanda, although the progress realised in the high numbers of women represented in governance institutions and processes is rooted in a range of affirmative-action policies adopted by the new post-genocide government. However, when the high representation of women in the

Rwandan Parliament is put to the test across all security-related areas in Rwanda, this trend is not sustained. Careful research is, however, required to see the extent to which this is the case.

Overall, across these countries, the contents of the NAPs varies significantly and there is no clarity about how to measure progress in the absence of monitoring frameworks or indicators. However, it may very well be that UNSCR 1889 (2009), which calls for better data collection and reporting, could be used for this purpose. In sum, there is no real pattern at the national level which indicates a qualitative shift towards the introduction of gender perspectives in peace and security matters and processes. The expectation that regional actors and member states will be able to make a positive change in the practice of institutions and society is far from being fulfilled.

Conclusion

This paper has highlighted that the adoption of UNSCR 1325 on women, peace and security was enabled by the point of convergence of three pillars – feminist security analysis, civil society activism, and policy decision-making. These pillars, it argues, when working in harmony are able to bring about meaningful change in gender equality. However, they are often disconnected and this enables gender to be reduced to an 'add-on' in much of the peace and security discourse and/or to be marginalised in global security concerns. Moreover, in the application of UNSCR 1325 in Africa there has been little convergence between these pillars of influence.

The absence of a cohesive narrative that moves Africa towards the transformation of gender relations in peace and security processes therefore remains glaring. UN interventions are simply taken as part of a general process of peacebuilding; they do not often transform relationships and institutions in-country toward gender equality. Regional organisations and national governments have also not demonstrated an adequate commitment to a qualitative shift in gender inequality on the ground.

The three pillars of influence discussed in this article, at least in part, offer some promise and potential to qualitatively shift the continent toward the agenda of gender equality; but only if they genuinely converge. The recipe for convergence appears reachable but the disabling factors are seemingly entrenched and will require careful dismantling if the desired change is to be realised. As the adoption of UNSCR 1325 has demonstrated, a critical factor in the convergence of these pillars was that all three actors maintained an activist stance. Academics were numbered in the coalition for UNSCR 1325, as were key policy actors.

Ultimately, activism is the common denominator that provides much-needed momentum towards change. When the three pillars are pitched against each other and there is no unity of purpose, achieving impact-making change becomes a challenge. In addition to growing scholarship on gender and security in Africa, it is clear that academics must engage in measured activism, as must policy practitioners with the right credentials to influence change. This has emerged as an important factor in both policy development and application. These ingredients are a necessary driving force behind a change-making movement for gender equality in Africa and elsewhere.

Notes

1 See, for example, C Enloe, *The morning after: sexual politics at the end of the Cold War*, Berkeley, CA: University of California Press, 1993; JA Tickner, *Gender in international relations: feminist perspectives in achieving global security*, New York,

NY: Columbia University Press, 1992; JA Tickner, You just don't understand: troubled engagement between feminists and IR theorists, *International Studies Quarterly*, 41, 1997.

2 Falling into this category, for example, are the Convention on the Elimination of All Forms of Discrimination Against Women (CEDAW) and the Beijing Platform for Action, both of which predate the first UNSC Resolution (1325) to deal with unequal security for women as well as gender inequality in peace and security related processes.

3 These three pillars were first identified in an article by two of the authors of the present article; see 'F Olonisakin and C Hendricks, Engaging (in)security as an entry point for seeking redress in gender inequality in Africa, *Africa Peace and Conflict Journal*, 6, 2013.

4 See, for example, C Enloe, *The morning after: sexual politics at the end of the Cold War*, Berkeley, CA: University of California Press, 1993; JA Tickner, *Gender in international relations: feminist perspectives in achieving global security*, New York, NY: Columbia University Press, 1992; JA Tickner, You just don't understand: troubled engagement between feminists and IR theorists, *International Studies Quarterly*, 41, 1997; I Skjelbaek, *Gendered battlefields: a gender analysis of peace and conflict*, PRIO Report 6/97, Oslo: International Peace Research Institute 1997; EM Blanchard, Gender, international relations and the development of feminist security theory: a review essay, *Signs: Journal of Women in Culture and Society*, 28, 2001.

5 See, for example, MW Segal, Women's military roles cross-nationally: past, present and future, *Gender and Society*, 9, 1995; C Cockburn and D Zarkov (eds.), *The postwar moment: militaries, masculinities and international peacekeeping – Bosnia and the Netherlands*, London: Lawrence and Wishart, 2002.

6 See CM Hendricks, *Gender and security in Africa*, Discussion Paper 63, Uppsala: Nordic Africa Institute, 2011, 5. See also C Enloe, *Bananas, beaches and bases: making feminist sense of international politics*, Berkeley, CA: University of California Press, 1989; C Enloe, All the men are in the militias, all the women are victims, in LA Lorentzen and J Turpin (eds.), *The women and war reader*, New York, NY: New York University Press, 1998; V Peterson (ed.), *Gendered states: feminist (re)visions on international relations theory*, Boulder, CO: Lynne Rienner, 1992; JA Tickner, *Gender in international relations: feminist perspectives in achieving global security*, New York, NY: Columbia University Press, 1992.

7 K Booth and J Baylis, *Britain, N.A.T.O and nuclear weapons: alternative defence versus alliance reform*, London: Palgrave Macmillan, 1989.

8 CM Hendricks, *Gender and security in Africa*, Discussion Paper 63, Uppsala: Nordic Africa Institute, 2011, 6.

9 See, for example, B Buzan, *People, states and fear: an agenda for international security studies in the post-Cold War era*, Boulder, CO: Lynne Rienner, 1991.

10 H Hudson, Doing security as though humans matter: a feminist perspective on gender and the politics of human security, *Security Dialogue*, 36, 2005.

11 Among many of his publications, see J Galtung, *Essays in peace research*, New Jersey: Humanities Press, 1975.

12 KE Boulding, *Stable peace*, Austin: University of Texas Press, 1978.

13 K Booth, *Security and self: reflections of a fallen realist*, YCISS Occasional Paper No. 26, York Centre for International and Strategic Studies, 1994.

14 United Nations Development Programme, *Human development report*, New York: Oxford University Press, 1994.

15 See, for example, M Nuruzzaman, Paradigms in conflict: the contested claims of human security, critical theory and feminism, *Cooperation and Conflict*, 41, 2006.

16 H Hudson, Doing security as though humans matter: a feminist perspective on gender and the politics of human security, *Security Dialogue*, 36, 2005, 157.

17 D Lewis, Rethinking human security: the implications for gender mainstreaming, in C Hendricks (ed.), *From state security to human security in southern Africa: policy research and capacity building challenges*, ISS Monograph 122, Pretoria: Institute for Security Studies, 2006, 9.

18 H Hudson, Doing security as though humans matter: a feminist perspective on gender and the politics of human security, *Security Dialogue*, 36, 2005.

19 See, for example, special issue on Militarism, Conflict and Women's Activism in *Feminist Africa* Issue 10 2008; 'F Olonisakin and A Okech (eds.), *Women and security governance in Africa*, Oxford: Pambazuka Press, 2011.

20 See 'F Olonisakin and C Hendricks, Engaging (in)security as an entry point for seeking redress in gender inequality in Africa, *Africa Peace and Conflict Journal*, 6, 2013.

21 See K Barnes, The evolution and implementation of UNSCR 1325: an overview, in 'F Olonisakin, K Barnes, and E Ikpe (eds.), *Women, peace and security: translating policy into practice*, London: Routledge, 2011.

22 C Cohn, Mainstreaming gender in UN security policy: a path to political transformation?, in SM Rai and G Waylen (eds.), *Global governance: feminist perspectives*, Basingstoke: Palgrave Macmillan, 2008.

23   The United Nations Transitional Assistance Group, The Windhoek Declaration and Namibia Plan of Action, 2000, http://www.un.org/womenwatch/osagi/wps/windhoek_declaration.pdf (accessed March 2013).

24   See C Hendricks, Framing the issues, in C Hendricks and M Chivasa (eds.), *ISS Women and Peacebuilding Workshop report*, Institute for Security Studies, Pretoria, 2009, 10.

25   F Hill, C Cohn, and C Enloe, *UN Security Council Resolution 1325 three years on: gender, security and organizational change*, Boston Centre for Gender in Organisations, Simmons School of Management, Consortium Lecture January 20, 2004.

26   See K Barnes, The evolution and implementation of UNSCR 1325: an overview, in 'F Olonisakin, K Barnes, and E Ikpe (eds.), *Women, peace and security: translating policy into practice*, London: Routledge, 2011, 19–20. See also C Cohn, Mainstreaming gender in UN security policy: a path to political transformation?, in SM Rai and G Waylen (eds.), *Global governance: feminist perspectives*, Basingstoke: Palgrave Macmillan, 2008.

27   Nearly all UN peace operations since the early 2000s have included the implementation of UNSCR 1325 in their mandates in one form or another. In Africa, this currently includes the UN Mission in Liberia (UNMIL), the UN Mission in Sudan (UNMIS), the UN AU Mission in Dafur (UNAMID), the UN Mission in the Congo (MONUC), and the UN Operation in Cote d'Ivoire (UNOCI).

28   See, for example, EN Wamai, UNSCR 1325 implementation in Liberia: dilemmas and challenges, in in 'F Olonisakin, K Barnes, and E Ikpe (eds.), *Women, peace and security: translating policy into practice*, London: Routledge, 2011; G Eltahir-Eltom, The impact of UNSCR 1325 and peacekeeping operations in Sudan, in 'F Olonisakin, K Barnes, and E Ikpe (eds.), *Women, peace and security: translating policy into practice*, London: Routledge, 2011.

29   This view is based on observations made on various peace operations. Between them, the authors have conducted field visits in the last decade to conflict-affected and/or peace operations environments in Liberia, Sierra Leone, the Democratic Republic of Congo, Sudan and Somalia.

30   African Union, Solemn Declaration on Gender Equality, Addis Ababa, 2004.

31   Discussion with ECOWAS officials in Abuja at the ECOWAS Partners' Meeting, April 2013

32   R Musa, *Evaluation of the implementation of the Solemn Declaration on Gender Equality in Africa, Senegal: Gender in My Agenda Campaign/ Femmes Africa Solidarite*, 2009.

33   Interview conducted with AMISOM officials by 'F Olonisakin, Mogadishu, 2 May 2013.

34   See Chapter 8 on Conflict Resolution and Peace Building in the annual editions (2010–2015) of C Lowe Morna, S Dube and L Makamure (eds.) SADC Gender Protocol Barometer, Johannesburg: Gender Links. The chapter is compiled by C Hendricks in the various annual editions of the SADC Gender Protocol Barometer.

35   United Nations, Report of the Secretary-General on Women, Peace and Security, S/2004/814, New York, 2004.

36   K Barnes, The evolution and implementation of UNSCR 1325: an overview, in 'F Olonisakin, K Barnes, and E Ikpe (eds.), *Women, peace and security: translating policy into practice*, London: Routledge, 2011, 26.

Women combatants and the liberation movements in South Africa

Guerrilla girls, combative mothers and the in-betweeners

Siphokazi Magadla

This article examines women's role as combatants in national liberation forces in South Africa. Three categories – guerrilla girls, combative mothers and the in-betweeners – are introduced to underscore the varied ways in which women have participated in combat within the national liberation movements. Factors such as age and one's ability to leave the country affected whether women could participate in combat as 'guerrilla girls' or if it limited them to fighting apartheid violence from home, or if there were women who can be defined as having fallen somewhere in between these categories. These categories are used to theorise women's combat roles in the anti-apartheid struggle, thus broadening and challenging the dominant notions of combat that often hide women's contributions in war. In this regard, different periods of struggle, physical location, as well as age, determined the methods of activism available to men and women.

Introduction

The establishment of the Department of Military Veterans in 2009 by the Jacob Zuma administration, and the subsequent adoption of the Military Veterans Act No. 18 of 2011, signalled a re-emergence of the combatant into post-apartheid public culture. Since 1994, the legacy of the country's militarised past had largely been subsumed under the Department of Defence, which was responsible for coordinating programmes to assist demobilised soldiers' transition into civilian life. Writing in the Cape Times, Dzinesa argued that

> President Jacob Zuma's reorganisation of South Africa's defence ministry into the Ministry of Defence and Military Veterans, which is also tasked with the concerns of war veterans, is a recognition of the important place this group occupies in the body politic.[1]

For Dzinesa, this reconfigured visibility of veterans' issues by the state pointed to a recognition that 'thousands of South Africa's former liberation fighters are unemployed, lead destitute lives and suffer psycho-social problems'.[2] Furthermore, he argues that the state was also reacting to anxieties that if veterans' socio-political issues are not addressed, 'their military training may cause – and in many cases has, in fact, caused – destitute veterans to turn to crime or become mercenaries'.[3] This view, that the majority of individuals who participated militarily in the anti-apartheid struggle now lead destitute lives, dominates the literature on former combatants in South Africa.[4]

This article pays close attention to women's role as combatants in national liberation forces. The military veteran discourses in post-apartheid South Africa make visible the ways in which the participation of women in combat has been confined to orthodox definitions of combat that do not account for the context that structured the ways in which women participated. The unconventional nature of apartheid violence limits the extent to which the Department of Defence can facilitate veterans' concerns where both the combatant and the veteran defy conventional definitions. The limited literature that examines women's roles in war, especially the contribution of Jacklyn Cock, can be understood as forming part of the feminist literature that locates women's contributions within the logic of state and guerrilla armies, which defines combat in battle-centric ways.[5] While this literature is useful in challenging dominant views about women's capacity to compete in these domains with men, it however risks narrowing women's extensive and nuanced contributions. Therefore, fresh analyses on women's combat roles in the national liberation movements need to reflect the contextual realities of their lives and the ways in which apartheid, as an unconventional war, blurred the distinctions between battlefront and home front, as well as combatant and civilian.

Three categories – guerrilla girls, combative mothers and the in-betweeners – are introduced to underscore the varied ways in which women participated in combat within the national liberation movements. It is suggested that factors such as age and one's ability to leave the country affected whether women could participate in combat as 'guerrilla girls' or if they were limited to fighting apartheid violence from home, or if there were women who can be defined as having fallen somewhere in between these categories. It is further suggested that these categories can be useful in theorising women's combat roles in the anti-apartheid struggle, because paying attention to them allows one to broaden and challenge the dominant notions of combat that often hide women's contributions in war. In this regard, different periods of struggle and physical location, as well as age, determined the methods of activism available to men and women.

The re-emergence of the combatant in public culture opens up a space within which to revisit women's roles in anti-apartheid violence and the ways in which their contribution is recognised in the state processes that award material benefits to those that are defined as military veterans. A more nuanced examination will allow us to judge the extent to which the state's renewed mission to support military veterans is framed in ways that define veteran status according to the realities of unconventional war for both women and men. This attention to context will contribute to the extent to which women combatants will benefit in the material rewards that are accorded to those who risked their lives to end apartheid.

A note on method

This article is part of a doctoral research project that examines the civilian integration of female ex-combatants in post-apartheid South Africa. The work seeks to fill a gap identifiable in the research on demobilisation and civilian integration of former combatants in South Africa. Whereas there is a vast literature in Africa and elsewhere that examines the socio-political and economic challenges that are faced by women who are former combatants in post-war societies – including Zimbabwe,[6] Eritrea,[7] Sudan,[8] Liberia,[9] Angola,[10] Uganda and Mozambique,[11] Sierra Leone,[12] and elsewhere – none of the major case studies conducted in South Africa since 1994 provide any detailed analysis of the plight of the demobilised female combatant.[13]

This study is based on a sample of 36 life histories of women who participated in different military formations that were aligned with the national liberation movements: the Umkhonto weSizwe (MK) of the African National Congress (ANC), the Azanian's People's Liberation Army (APLA) of the Pan Africanist Congress (PAC), and Amabutho, a self-defence unit (SDU) based in Port Elizabeth. Of the women interviewed, 18 belonged to the MK, 7 to the APLA, and 11 to Amabutho. The 36 women interviewed are between the ages of 46 and 88 years. The interviews were conducted over a period of 11 months, from July 2013 to May 2014, in Port Elizabeth, East London, Umthatha, Johannesburg and Pretoria, as well as five telephone interviews.

It is from these life histories that I make the argument that the examination of women's participation in combat within the national liberation movements needs to pay attention to the different spaces and methods women used to participate in combat, beyond the current emphasis on the combat role of the transnationally-trained guerrilla women. I wish to demonstrate that placing women in different categories provides a fresh and nuanced historical understanding of women's participation in the apartheid battle. It also offers the space to ask deeper questions about the ways in which these women have transitioned from militarised livelihoods in post-apartheid South Africa.

Women combatants in a transnational 'late twentieth-century' war

According to Ellis, 'what South Africa experienced in the late twentieth century was a civil war, fought among the people'.[14] This war 'resembled many other violent conflicts in the late twentieth century … The point was not so much to destroy the enemy as to win political support'.[15] Clausewitz's classic conception of war confines the activity of war to being between two or more states who seek to defend their territorial integrity and sovereignty from an outside threat.[16] This conception of military activity creates a sharp distinction between soldier and civilian. However, a key distinguishing factor of 'late twentieth-century' wars has been the blurring of the distinctions between the combatant and civilian. As Gear points out, in these wars 'combat is not a homogeneous experience' as it includes 'those who are not in the frontline'.[17] Although the definition of 'civil war' restricts the geography of violence to one particular state, most if not all civil wars have transnational dimensions. The anti-apartheid struggle is not different in this case, as national liberation movements such as the ANC, the PAC and the South Africa Communist Party (SACP) operated across borders. In so doing, they created substantial overlaps with the struggles inside South Africa, especially in terms of underground activity. The reaction of the apartheid state against a challenge to its policies was also transnational in nature.

Mao Tse-tung defines guerrilla war as 'a weapon that a nation inferior in arms and military equipment may employ against a more powerful aggressor nation'.[18] Guerrilla warfare should hence be understood as 'military strength organized by the active people and inseparable from them'.[19] Guerrilla warfare came to prominence in the post-Second World War era and 'was adopted in Africa as elsewhere as the most effective means of defeating the highly organized and heavily armed, but also cumbersome and alien armies of the major industrial powers and their local allies'.[20] Other examples of armed liberation movements include those in Guinea-Bissau, Angola and Mozambique, which led to the removal of Portuguese rule.

In terms of policy, the ANC defined its battle against the apartheid state in terms of 'four pillars' at the 1969 consultative conference in Morogoro, Tanzania. These four pillars consisted of: mass mobilisation, the establishment of underground structures, the armed struggle, and the mobilisation of the international community to support the struggle of the South African people and isolate the apartheid state. According to Barrell, the ANC and its ally the SACP 'were influenced by a number of revolutionary struggles … But none seems to have been quite as influential as the Cuban revolution'.[21] The founding document of the ANC's military army, MK, notes that 'as in Cuba, the general uprising must be sparked off by organized and well prepared guerrilla operations during the course of which the masses of the people will be drawn and armed'.[22] The violence thus involved a powerful state with a professional army facing a weaker force whose main asset was the arming of the ordinary population in what they labelled a 'protracted guerrilla war'.[23] As noted by Cock, the 'ANC's "People War" strategy, which was adopted in 1983, highlights the problem of a clear differentiation between combatants, and non-combatants that rests on a precise demarcation of the battlefield'.[24] In this regard Cock further argues that 'one of the defining features of South Africa as a country engaged in war is that the battlefield comprehends the entire society'.[25]

This is moreover complicated by the fact that the apartheid state did not acknowledge itself as engaged in a war. The apartheid state in the late 1970s saw itself as engaged in a 'total onslaught', preferring to refer to its 'enemy' as *terrorists* rather than declaring an outright war. According to Cock and Nathan, the choice for the apartheid state to define the conflict as unrest or terrorism as opposed to war implied that liberation movement fighters were denied the prisoner of war status granted by the Geneva Protocols to those engaged in war against colonial powers.[26] Dlamini argues that the apartheid's state's notion of total strategy was conceived by a French general and military strategist, Andre Beaufre, who had in the Second World War fought in Indochina and Algeria, and commanded the French forces during the 1956 Suez crisis.[27] According to Dlamini, 'Beaufre's idea, simply put, was that militaries needed to think of their battlefronts in total terms, meaning there should be no distinction between the civil and the military spheres'.[28]

The total strategy of the apartheid state erased the lines between militaristic and civil, thus blurring the lines between combatant and civilian. Endlmann argues that the apartheid state's 'total onslaught' ideology 'ensured that the National Party government worked at drawing every white South African into its efforts to counteract the perceived threats of communism and African nationalism'.[29] In this context, the compulsory conscription of all school-leaving white males from 1968 to 1993 'formed part of a broader social, political and ideological system of which every white South African was a part in one way or another'.[30]

Bozzoli, writing about the 'Six Day War' between residents and police in an Alexandra township in Johannesburg in February 1986, characterises this as 'the transformation of space into territory'.[31] As Endlmann points out with regard to the role of conscripts in the violence,

> a fact that is largely ignored in the memoirs about conscription is that conscripts also served alongside the police in South Africa's townships, the length and breadth of the country, as the government sought to quell the uprising of the Mass Democratic Movement. At the same time that the Border War was taking place, there was a civil war within South Africa.[32]

Bonnin, writing about the transformation of space during the political violence in KwaZulu-Natal between the ANC-aligned United Democratic Front (UDF) and the Inkatha Freedom Party (IFP), argues that 'spaces of everyday life were to be reterritorialized and new spaces and boundaries within the township recreated'.[33] Beall et al. argue similarly that the nature of apartheid violence was such that

> the site of struggle shifted to the home and community, into a sphere in which women have particular responsibility and which they feel particularly obliged to defend ... the home is traditionally regarded as the women's domain, and the care of children is 'women's work' .... Such tactics forced women to take positions in the front line of the battle and allowed them to assume leadership roles, laying the basis for a transformation of women's role and position in struggle: they are drawn in to defend their terrain but in so doing are forced to move beyond narrowly conceived notions of their roles.[34]

It is within this context that women's participation in combat should be understood. Elshtain argues that historically in the Euro-American imagination men and women have occupied distinct roles in the activity of war – women as 'noncombatants' and men as 'warriors'.[35] Women's access to combat has been a central aspect of women's struggles to attain full citizenship rights. Yuval-Davis argues that women's access to combat is important because it is linked to women's capacity to access citizenship, as it is believed that 'once women share with men the ultimate citizen's duty – to die for one's country, they would also be able to gain equal citizenship rights to those of men'.[36] This is because feminists have argued that international relations theory and practice is 'encoded as masculine territory' because 'the soldier, the citizen, the political subject, and the state are gendered male'.[37] Therefore, war offers a 'site for rudimentary change in relations between women and men'.[38]

Guerrilla girls

Cock's study of women in the MK and the South African Defence Force (SADF) remains the only book entirely focused on women's formal participation in statutory and non-statutory forces.[39] It examines the experiences of women in MK camps outside South Africa in comparison to those of white women who were soldiers in the SADF. Although the numbers of women in MK in exile changed throughout the different periods of struggle, little is written about their role in the 1960s, while their presence is better recorded in the 1970s and 1980s. The number of women involved increased after the 1976 student uprisings in Soweto. By 1991, women are said to have constituted 20% of MK membership.[40] Cock's study reveals that women were under-represented in positions of leadership and authority in MK, and this was true too in the parent body (ANC) more broadly.[41]

I use the term 'guerrilla girls' to point to the fact that the average woman who joined the MK was usually in her teens and early twenties. Only three of the 18 sampled MK women had been working professionals before leaving the country – two nurses and a teacher. With the exception of one woman who joined the MK in 1978, the women in this sample joined the MK between 1980 and 1987. They received minor to extensive military training in countries such as Swaziland, Tanzania, Lesotho, Angola, East Germany, Cuba and Russia. Most of them had participated in student politics, especially the Congress of South African Students (COSAS). Most reached the decision to leave the country due to constant police harassment and imprisonment that included torture. The feeling that there was no option but to leave the country is a constant narrative that is told by women who joined the MK:

> I was in solitary confinement close to a year in Port Elizabeth. And then after my release I went home and by the time I went home ... I felt ... okay, now I still needed to go back to school. When I went back there, I discovered that my name was scrapped off the roll. ... The education department had identified me or expelled me. So I started thinking deeply about this expulsion. When will it end as, I mean, I was also very conscious of being a woman without education. Remember, I enjoyed studying I had passion; I had ambition as a young African girl. So I was left with no choice but to leave South Africa. (MK ex-combatant, Port Elizabeth, 2013)

Intimate experiences with apartheid violence also influenced women's political consciousness and their ultimate decision to choose military training as a response to fighting against apartheid:

> The reason for me to join was that my mother was a businesswoman 'cause she had a shebeen selling vetkoeks, chicken, fish and all of that. Now from time to time police will come in, kick the doors, take everything, and I used to be very scared ... . This police business traumatised me, in fact, to an extent that when COSAS came into play, I was readily prepared to join it because they were saying the same things that I felt needed to be dealt with in terms of fighting the regime and of course doing away with corporal punishment because it was another way that they were instilling fear – the regime that is. So I readily joined COSAS. (MK ex-combatant, Johannesburg, 2014)

Another former combatant, who had also been active in COSAS, left the country following the killing of her brother by the apartheid security forces in Lesotho:

> In Tanzania a person would stay for six months in this place called Dakawa. Dakawa was a transit camp. Now, some of the people were staying at school because you were given an option there: you either want to go to school or you would indicate that you wanted to be trained as a soldier to go and fight. So at the time I chose that I would go and fight. I would train because I was so bitter, because my brother was the breadwinner at home [and] I realised that everyone was angry that they took away our breadwinner. I needed to avenge his death. So I decided to go to the army. (MK ex-combatant, Port Elizabeth, 2013)

As in Cock, the women emphasised that they received the same military training as their male counterparts and that they were able to compete on equal terms.[42] While prominent women such as Thandi Modise, Thenjiwe Mtitso and Mavis Nhlapho have spoken out about the persistent sexual harassment in ANC camps in Angola, where the males went unpunished by MK leadership for harassing women,[43] some women did confirm these unequal gender relations within the military camps, while several others were adamant that women entered into consensual relationships with their male counterparts:

> The one thing that I must really emphasise: during our time or my time we were growing up in a very protected environment. I must say I'm not speaking for somebody else or those before us because, again, I can confidently attest to the fact that we were highly protected as women – women of MK. In as much as we were called flowers of the revolution – the mighty few –

we were treated as equals through training, leading and every other way. But also our rights were protected. I'm raising this because, because there's been this saying that people were raped … not during our times. I will not speak for other people. We were sleeping in [the] open, there were no doors. We were never raped. Whatever you were doing it was a conscious decision. You were regarded as adults, of course, even if you were young, and therefore we were consenting adults. To an extent that during our time there is what was called order number 25. Order number 25, it was just saying as long as you are a recruit or a fresh … ikrusant as we were casually known when you are new, you cannot be involved or have a relationship, or a sexual relationship with trained personnel. This was done precisely so that those who have been there before us cannot take advantage of us; and should you be found doing that you will be punished, and severely so … . So I'm raising that because I've seen interviews, I've seen people talking for whatever reason. (MK ex-combatant, Johannesburg, 2014)

These views were expressed by the majority of the women I interviewed. It seems to me that women emphasised this point as a response to the fact that analyses of women in the MK often focus on women as unequal participants within the organisation, often with the danger of erasing the transformative impact that women had within the space in terms of altering conservative gender relations.

The emphasis on the experiences of camp life of women within the MK is the dominant depiction of women's trajectory in the MK. However, in the field I also encountered a woman who had participated in the MK at its founding, working with Govan Mbeki and Raymond Mhlaba in Port Elizabeth during the sabotage campaigns, where she worked as a courier of explosives. She reported that she has not received ex-combatant benefits because, in the absence of military training, her work contribution in the 1960s is not recognised. Thus there is also a need to explore different narratives of women within the MK whose role is different to that of the 'typical' guerrilla girl.

Combative mothers

Cherry has been critical of what she perceives as the privileging of the MK in narratives of the armed struggle.[44] She critiques the recognition of 'largely ineffective MK soldiers' materially and symbolically, compared to those 'who conducted the struggle at the cutting edge of the people's strategy in the townships [who] are the least recognised'.[45] Many of these formations saw themselves as carrying the mandate of the MK and APLA inside the country. Mokalobe for instance notes that 'senior MK combatants provided training to SDUs to defend communities against security forces and Inkatha. In KwaZulu-Natal, MK combatants such as Jeff Radebe and Sipho Sithole trained and armed the SDUs to protect communities against warlords in the townships'.[46] Cherry also examines the role of women in the heightened violence of the 1980s under the United Democratic Front (UDF) and the SDUs.[47] Cherry contends that 'in the mid 1980s, the mass movement came increasingly into a violent confrontation with the apartheid state [in] what came to be described as the "township uprising" [that] engulfed black communities in the period from 1984 to 1989'.[48] Cherry states that in the vast literature on the 'uprising' of the mid-1980s, 'there is scarcely a word written about the role played by women in this decisive period of struggle'.[49] Instead, gender-blind categories such as 'the people', 'youth', 'community', 'residents' and 'masses' are used. When the gender dynamics of the time are made visible, it becomes clear that it is young males in the townships who are perceived as having taken 'control of public space, while women were expected to provide shelter and guard their private space. Representations in writing, film and photography of the "young lions" almost always portrays the aggressive and macho young men confronting the state'.[50]

The informal structures known as the Amabutho in the Eastern Cape 'played the role both of confronting security forces and coercing residents in support of campaigns'.[51] Additionally, as Cherry notes, Amabutho were also known for taking 'brutal action against those deemed to be spies or collaborators with the apartheid government'.[52] Bonnin further argues that in this period 'the street became reconstructed as a site of masculine power'.[53] The image of this male youth is often juxtaposed with that of the older women whose mothering role became 'socially rather than biologically defined, since, in situations of conflict, any boy became the son of any woman'.[54] It is these older women that I was pointed to in Port Elizabeth when I was searching for women who had participated on the side of the Amabutho. The political role is often documented under the Port Elizabeth Black Civic Organisation (PEBCO), an affiliate of UDF, as well as the Port Elizabeth Women's Organisation (PEWO). Their role in 'protecting' the young men from the police often placed them at the direct line of danger:

> One night a bullet came through the window. Twaa! It hit the wall, the wall in the kitchen. We were protected by God because I cannot tell you how we survived. I was cooking, making supper. Twaa! I reasoned that he was shooting at us; he wanted my life as well. I used to be woken up all the time by the Boers. They were looking for the young men. They would wake them up, beat them and leave with them…that is the life we lived. (Interview in Port Elizabeth, 2013)

Although scholars such as Wells and Walker have been critical of black women's use of 'maternal politics' in the national liberation movements,[55] it is important to examine women's roles under the 'political and social conditions that structured their lives and how this exerted a profound influence on their chosen methods of activism as well as on the ways in which they perceived their experiences'.[56] I argue that the literature on women's combat roles in the liberation movements needs to account for the central role played by women in different roles, including the ways in which motherhood shaped how they participated in the violence that structured daily life under apartheid. Similarly, Soiri notes that the apartheid regime in Namibia 'threatened the lives of children in homes and at schools. The family became then the most effective site of resistance and support'.[57]

Perhaps we can argue that the misrecognition of women's contribution in pushing back against the violence of the 1980s is connected to the misrecognition of the 'young lions' in that their participation against the state was deeply rooted in the defence of their communities, which was enabled by the support that they received from their mothers: this has been negated. Therefore, by taking women's contributions seriously in these domains, we can begin to understand the deep structural roots of the anti-apartheid struggle for all those who were involved. We have to wonder, would the 'People's War' of the 1980s, which rendered the country ungovernable, been successful if community resources had not been marshalled to fight back through the participation of women?

The in-betweeners

While older women played this role under organisations such as the PEBCO and PEWO, little mention has been made about the role of young women at this time beyond also caring for the male youth as their 'little sisters'.[58] Cherry notes that the role of young women who were members of the COSAS and the Port Elizabeth Youth Congress (PEYCO) played a crucial role in bridging the gap between parents and the youth.[59] As Seekings argues, 'younger women were motivated to join student and or youth organizations because of their specific concerns and experiences', such as conditions in school, while 'these organizations did not have the same attraction to slightly older women who had left school'.[60] Yet, beyond these specific needs, young women also laboured hard to bridge the gap between the young and old. They 'would try to convince the "mothers" about the importance of school boycotts, trying to explain the need for political organisation and resistance, and support for their children in the pursuance of political objectives'.[61] With regard to increased state violence in the townships from 1984 onwards, Cherry argues that women are represented either as

> the passive or innocent victims of male violence, or defenders of home and children. The reality of women's experiences was more complex and varied than this, however. While it can be said that the response of the older township women to the escalating violence was primarily defensive ... young women were in certain situations able to play the roles normally assigned only to men – *of aggressors or combatants*. In addition, there were strategies adopted which blurred the line between offensive and defensive action, and introduced women to leadership roles as the conflict escalated.[62]

I categorise these women as the 'in-betweeners' – because they occupy a space between the 'combative mothers' and the guerrilla girls – who had been active in the student movement in the country and then eventually left the country. The women I spoke to participated in Amabutho as marshals who, with their male counterparts, were responsible for securing public gatherings such as funerals and public protests. All of them had offered the 'guard of honour' at the funeral of The Cradock Four in 1985. One of the women gave birth following a violent hit to the stomach at another funeral in Port Elizabeth. Another woman who had been a marshal insisted that 'you felt apartheid on your body', pointing to the constant violence that they faced under the state. Some of the women spoke about the impacts of their political involvement, as some of them never finished school due to constant police harassment. Many of them find themselves unable to compete in the post-apartheid political economy due to the sacrifices that they made during the height of the violence of the 1980s. The economic challenges are coupled with palatable psychological trauma due to memories of violence and death.

It seems to me that a sustained engagement with women's combatant roles in the liberation struggle needs to account for the ways in which women responded to the battlefront that was daily life under apartheid. A narrow focus on the few women who were able to physically escape for military training outside the country only offers one lens on the ways in which women in South Africa were thrust into battle. Close attention to these various women allows us to ask nuanced questions about their well-being in post-apartheid South Africa.

Policy implications

The re-emergence of the 'military veteran' as a legislative category that seeks to symbolically and materially reward South Africans who participated in anti-apartheid violence invites questions about the nature of military contestation during apartheid. According to the Military Veterans Act, a military veteran is a South African citizen who:

> (a) rendered military service to any of the military organisations, statutory and non-statutory; which were involved on all sides of South Africa's Liberation War from 1960 to 1994; (b) served in the Union Defence Force before 1961; or (c) became a member of the new South African National Defence Force after 1994, and has completed his or her military training and no longer performs military service, and has not been dishonourably discharged from that military organization or force.[63]

In this frame, therefore, veteran status is confined to membership in a military organisation, whereas the majority of those who participated in the armed struggle did not officially belong to a military organisation. This reflects the frame of the 1993–94 integration and demobilisation process led by the Joint Military Coordinating Committee (JMCC), which consisted of representatives from the statutory forces, the 'SADF and the armed forces of the nominally independent homelands of the Transkei, Bophuthatswana, Venda and Ciskei (TBVC)', while the non-statutory forces were composed of the MK and APLA.[64] As noted by van der Merwe and Lamb, the 'CPR-based SANDF integration and demobilised process was integral in defining who constitutes South African ex-combatants'.[65] Amongst those excluded were the paramilitary formations that operated inside South African townships such as the self-protection units of the IFP and the SDUs.[66]

This is in contrast to countries such as Namibia, where the definition of veteran is defined as 'any person who was a member of the liberation forces who consistently and persistently participated or engaged in any political, diplomatic or underground activity in furtherance of the liberation struggle, or was arrested for such activities'.[67] As Metsoala argues, this expansion of the veteran category in Namibia has 'brought more gender balance to reintegration, as the exile division of labour placed women mainly in supportive functions and not in actual combat'.[68] In the sample of women interviewed for this study, the women who participated in the demobilisation process, who benefited from the demobilisation packages and who are receiving the veterans' monthly pension are the transnationally trained 'guerrilla girls'. Even though not all of them are receiving the monthly pension, none of the women who participated internally were able to participate in the demobilisation process and none of them are receiving the pension, housing, health and education benefits that are due to veterans.

Conclusion

The re-emergence of the combatant in public culture allows for an important intersection between the past and the present. In this article, I aimed to demonstrate that women's roles in the armed struggle need to be understood in line with the varied ways in which women were affected by apartheid violence. I aimed to demonstrate that the trained transnational female guerrilla does not fully encapsulate the complex ways in which women were thrust into combat. By locating women in these different spaces and creating new categories, as I do here, it may be possible to examine whether the state's present commitment to supporting those who participated in combat pays attention to the unconventional nature of the apartheid battlefront. The discussion on 'combative mothers' and the 'in-betweeners' demonstrates that it is not only women's contribution to the fight for liberation that is at stake, but rather that a misrecognition of many others who risked their lives fighting apartheid may today not be recognised as legitimate.

Acknowledgements

I would like to thank my supervisor, Professor Paul Bischoff, for his ongoing support on this thesis project. I would also like thank colleagues at the Center for African Studies at the University of California, Berkeley, and African Studies at Ohio University – where I presented in March 2015 – and the Gender and Security in Africa conference hosted by the Institute for Security Studies in June 2015, where I shared the ideas presented in this article. Lastly, I am thankful to Gcobani Qambela and Lyn Ossome for their comments.

Funding

This publication was made possible by support from the Social Science Research Council's Next Generation Social Sciences in Africa Felloswhip Program, with funds provided by the Carnegie Corporation of New York.

Notes

1 G Dzinesa, Attention to the welfare of war veterans can prevent threats to stability, *Cape Times*, 15 July 2009, www.ccr. org.za/index.php/media-release/in-the-media/newspaper-articles/item/277-pr-115

2 *Ibid.*

3 *Ibid.*

4 I Liebenberg and M Roefs, *Demobilisation and its aftermath II: economic reinsertion of South Africa's demobilised military personnel*, Pretoria: Institute for Security Studies, 2001; MP Mokalobe, Demobilisation, reintegration, rationalisation and peacebuilding in South Africa, Master's thesis, University of Cape Town, 2001; S Gear, *Wishing us away: challenges facing ex-combatants in the 'new' South Africa*, Johannesburg: Centre for the Study of Violence and Reconciliation, 2002; Centre for Conflict Resolution, *Soldiers of misfortune*, unpublished research report, 2003; D Everatt (ed.), *Only useful until democracy? Reintegrating ex-combatants in South Africa (and lessons learned from Zimbabwe and Kosovo)*, New York, NY: Atlantic Philanthropies, 2006; L Mashike, *Former combatants' involvement in crime and crime prevention*, Johannesburg: Centre for the Study of Violence and Reconciliation, 2007.

5 J Cock, *Colonels and cadres: war and gender in South Africa*. Cape Town: Oxford University Press, 1991.

6 T Lyons, *Guns and guerilla girls: women in the Zimbabwean national liberation struggle*, Trenton: Africa World Press, 2004.

7 V Bernal, Equality to die for?: Women guerrilla fighters and Eritrea's cultural revolution, *Political and Legal Anthropology Review*, 23:2, 2000.

8 AA Halim, Attack with a friendly weapon, in M Turshen & C Twagiramanya (eds.), *What women do in war time: gender and conflict in Africa*, London: Zed Books, 1998.

9 Y Clarke, Security sector reform in Africa: a lost opportunity to deconstruct militarised masculinities?, *Feminist Africa*, 10, 2008; T Jaye, *Transitional justice and DDR: the case of Liberia*, New York: International Center for Transitional Justice, 2009.

10 V Farr, The importance of a gender perspective to successful disarmament, demobilization and reintegration processes, *Disarmament Forum*, 4, 2003.

11 S McKay and S Mazurana, *Where are the girls? Girls in fighting forces in northern Uganda, Sierra Leone and Mozambique: their lives during and after war*, Montreal: Rights & Democracy, 2004; M Tse-tung, *On guerrilla warfare*, Champaign, IL: University of Illinois Press, 1961.

12 C Coulter, Female fighters in the Sierra Leone war: challenging the assumptions?, *Feminist Review*, 88, 2008.

13 J Cock, *Colonels and cadres: war and gender in South Africa*. Cape Town: Oxford University Press, 1991; Liebenberg and M Roefs, *Demobilisation and its aftermath II: economic reinsertion of South Africa's demobilised military personnel*, Pretoria: Institute for Security Studies, 2001; MP Mokalobe, Demobilisation, reintegration, rationalisation and peacebuilding in South Africa, Master's thesis, University of Cape Town, South Africa, 2001; S Gear, *Wishing us away: challenges facing ex-combatants in the 'new' South Africa*, Johannesburg: Centre for the Study of Violence and Reconciliation, 2002; Centre for

Conflict Resolution, *Soldiers of misfortune*, unpublished research report, 2003; D Everatt (ed.), *Only useful until democracy? Reintegrating ex-combatants in South Africa (and lessons learned from Zimbabwe and Kosovo)*, New York, NY: Atlantic Philanthropies, 2006; L Mashike, *Former combatants' involvement in crime and crime prevention*, Johannesburg: Centre for the Study of Violence and Reconciliation, 2007; H van der Merwe & G Lamb, Transitional justice and DDR: the case of South Africa, 2009, https://ictj.org/sites/default/files/ICTJ-DDR-South-Africa-CaseStudy-2009-English.pdf (accessed 8 July 2015); G Maringir and J Brankovic, *The persistence of military identities among ex-combatants in South Africa*, Cape Town: Centre for the Study of Violence and Reconciliation and Centre for Humanities Research, 2013; L Heinecken & H Bwalya, Compensating military veterans in South Africa: what if we cannot pay the bill?, *African Security Review*, 22:1, 2013.

14 S Ellis, *External mission: the ANC in exile, 1960–1990*, Oxford: Oxford University Press, 2012, 291.

15 *Ibid.*, 278.

16 CV Clausewitz, *On war: the complete edition*, Rockville, MD: Wildside Press, 2009, 24.

17 S Gear, Wishing us away:challenges facing ex-combatants in the 'new' South Africa, Johannesburg: Centre for the Study of Violence and Reconciliation, 2002, 2.

18 M Tse-tung, *On guerrilla warfare*, Champaign, IL: University of Illinois Press, 1961, 42.

19 *Ibid*, 50.

20 CS Clapham (ed.), *African guerrillas*, Suffolk: James Currey, 2.

21 H Barrell, The turn to the masses: the African National Congress strategic review of 1978–79, *Journal of Southern African Studies*, 18, 1992, 69.

22 African National Congress, Operation Mayibuye, 1963, www.anc.org.za/show.php?id=4699 (accessed 8 July 2015).

23 T Lodge, *Black politics in South Africa since 1945*, David Phillip: Cape Town & Johannesburg, 1986, 236.

24 J Cock, Introduction, in J Cock & L Nathan (eds.), *War and society: the militarisation of South Africa*, South Africa: New Africa Books, 1989, 2.

25 *Ibid.*

26 J Cock & L Nathan (eds.), *War and society: the militarisation of South Africa*, South Africa: New Africa Books, 1989.

27 J Dlamini, *Askari: a story of collaboration and betrayal in the anti-apartheid struggle*, Johannesburg: Jacana Media, 2014.

28 *Ibid.*, 105

29 T Endlmann, Negotiating historical continuities in contested terrain: a narrative-based reflection on the post-apartheid psychosocial legacies of conscription into the South African Defence Force, PhD dissertation, Rhodes University, Grahamstown, South Africa, 2014, 1.

30 *Ibid.*

31 B Bozzoli, *Theatres of struggle and the end of apartheid*, Athens, OH: Ohio University Press, 2004, 7–11.

32 T Endlmann, Negotiating historical continuities in contested terrain: a narrative-based reflection on the post-apartheid psychosocial legacies of conscription into the South African Defence Force, PhD dissertation, Rhodes University, Grahamstown, South Africa, 2014, 2–3.

33 D Bonnin, Claiming spaces, changing places: political violence and women's protests in KwaZulu-Natal, *Journal of Southern African Studies*, 26, 2000, 307.

34 Quoted in J Cherry, We were not afraid: the role of women in the 1980s township uprising in the Eastern Cape, in N Gasa (ed.), *Women in South African history: basusifimbokodo, bawel'imilambo/they remove boulders and cross rivers*, Pretoria: HSRC Press, 2007, 301.

35 JB Elshtain, *Women and war*, Chicago, IL: University of Chicago Press, 1987.

36 N Yuval-Davis, Women, citizenship and difference, *Feminist Review*, 57, 1997, 20.

37 J Pettman, *Worlding women: a feminist international politics*, London: Routledge, 1996, viii.

38 C Enloe, *Does khaki become you? The militarization of women's lives*, London: Pandora, 1983, 70.

39 J Cock, *Colonels and cadres: war and gender in South Africa*, Cape Town: Oxford University Press, 1991.

40 J Cock, *Colonels and cadres: war and gender in South Africa*, Cape Town: Oxford University Press, 1991; S Hassim, *The ANC Women's League: sex, politics and gender*, Johannesburg: Jacana Media, 2014.

41 J Cock, *Colonels and cadres: war and gender in South Africa*, Cape Town: Oxford University Press, 1991.

42 *Ibid.*

43 T Modise & R Curnow, Thandi Modise, a woman in war, *Agenda*, 43, 2000; S Hassim, *The ANC Women's League: sex, politics and gender*, Johannesburg: Jacana Media, 2014.

44 J Cherry, *Umkhonto weSizwe: a Jacana pocket history*, Johannesburg: Jacana Media, 2011.

45 *Ibid.*, 156–157.

46 MP Mokalobe, Demobilisation, reintegration, rationalisation and peacebuilding in South Africa, Master's thesis, University of Cape Town, South Africa, 2001, 133.

47 J Cherry, We were not afraid: the role of women in the 1980s township uprising in the Eastern Cape, in N Gasa (ed.), *Women in South African history: basus'ifimbokodo, bawel'imilambo/they remove boulders and cross rivers*, Pretoria: HSRC Press, 2007.

48 *Ibid.*, 262.

49 *Ibid.*

50 *Ibid.*, 291.

51 *Ibid.*

52 *Ibid.*, 308.

53 D Bonnin, Claiming spaces, changing places: political violence and women's protests in KwaZulu-Natal, *Journal of Southern African Studies*, 26, 2000, 309.

54 *Ibid.*

55 J Wells, The rise and fall of motherism as a force in black women's resistance movements, paper presented at the Conference on Gender in Southern Africa, University of Natal, Durban, 1991; C Walker, Conceptualising motherhood in twentieth century South Africa, *Journal of Southern African Studies*, 21, 1995.

56 Z Magubane, Attitudes towards feminism among women in the ANC, 1950–1990: a theoretical re-interpretation, in S Ndlovu (ed.), *The Road to democracy in South Africa: volume 4 (1980–1990)*, Pretoria: UNISA Press, 2010, 996.

57 I Soiri, *The radical motherhood: Namibian women's independence struggle*, Uppsala: Nordic Africa Institute, 1996, 91.

58 D Bonnin, Claiming spaces, changing places: political violence and women's protests in KwaZulu-Natal, *Journal of Southern African Studies*, 26, 2000, 309.

59 J Cherry, We were not afraid: the role of women in the 1980s township uprising in the Eastern Cape, in N Gasa (ed.), *Women in South African history: basus'ifimbokodo, bawel'imilambo/they remove boulders and cross rivers*, Pretoria: HSRC Press, 2007.

60 J Seekings, 'Gender Ideology and Township Politics in the 1980s', Agenda, 7:10, 1991, 81.

61 J Cherry, We were not afraid: the role of women in the 1980s township uprising in the Eastern Cape, in N Gasa (ed.), *Women in South African history: basus'ifimbokodo, bawel'imilambo/they remove boulders and cross rivers*, Pretoria: HSRC Press, 2007, 285.

62 *Ibid.*, 300, emphasis added.

63 Republic of South Africa Military Veterans Act No 18 of 2011 Assented to 5 December 2011 (http://www.dmv.gov.za/documents/The%20Military%20Veterans%20Act%20of%202011.pdf)

64 T Motumi & A Hudson, Rightsizing: the challenges of demobilization and social reintegration in South Africa, in J Cilliers (ed.), *Dismissed: demobilisation and reintegration of former combatants in Africa*, Pretoria: Institute for Security Studies, 1995, 113.

65 H van der Merwe & G Lamb, Transitional justice and DDR: the case of South Africa, 2009, 10, https://ictj.org/sites/default/files/ICTJ-DDR-South-Africa-CaseStudy-2009-English.pdf (accessed 8 July 2015).

66 L Mashike, *Former combatants' involvement in crime and crime prevention*, Johannesburg: Centre for the Study of Violence and Reconciliation, 2007; J Cherry, *Umkhonto weSizwe: a Jacana pocket history*, Johannesburg: Jacana Media, 2011.

67 L Heinecken & H Bwalya, Compensating military veterans in South Africa: what if we cannot pay the bill?, *African Security Review*, 22:1, 2013, 33.

68 L Metsola, 'Reintegration' of ex-combatants and former fighters: a lens into state formation and citizenship in Namibia, *Third World Quarterly*, 27, 2006, 1129.

Feminine masculinities in the military

The case of female combatants in the Kenya Defence Forces' operation in Somalia

Mokua Ombati

Historically, the military presents more defined gender boundaries than any other state institution. Assignment to traditionally non-feminine roles means crossing gender-assigned and constructed boundaries. This article explores the interplay of the contra-dictory dynamics of gender in the military through the lens of Kenyan women comba-tants in the war against al-Shabaab insurgents in Somalia. Military combat roles have traditionally relied on and manipulated ideas about masculinity and femininity. The study uses the twin theoretical frameworks of sociocultural capital and cultural scripts, refined by a gender-framing perspective, to interpret the sociocultural attitudes of masculinity and femininity in terms of war, the military and militarism.

Introduction

The military is a significant institution in the provision of national security, as a symbol of nation-hood and as a source of national identity. It occupies a special place in the public realm, somehow more intimately bound to patriotism, to the fate and dignity of the nation, than other public insti-tutions. However, the military remains fundamentally gendered. The military contributes to national and cultural definitions of what it means to be a man by furthering a 'cult of masculinity', as defined by the warrior hero. This 'cult of masculinity', which includes constructions of accep-table gender roles, is embedded within a 'combat, masculine-warrior paradigm'.[1]

In spite of the integration of women into the military, it is still the case that soldiering, violence and wars typify masculinity.[2] The military and militarism provide the moral, legal and even meta-physical justification, freedom and symbolism for the expression of that which is distinctly mascu-line. Notions of masculinity are powerful tools in the process of making soldiers.[3] Military formations are constructed around a particular form of masculinity that idealises raw power, strength, lethal force, aggression, competitiveness, censure of emotional expression and the creation and dehumanisation of the 'enemy'.[4] Militarism feeds into ideologies of masculinity through the eroticisation of stoicism, risk-taking, physical toughness, boldness and endurance. Militarisation is also variously expressed in such masculine attributes as self-discipline, professionalism, sociability, overt heterosexual desire, protection and decisiveness, individualism, rationality and practicality, courage and semblance of comradeship, cruelty, mindlessness, blind obedience and clannishness.[5]

In addition, traditional understandings of masculinity and femininity grant agency to male soldiers, regardless of their military role, by normalising the image of the combative soldier as man and ensuring that infantry women remain liminal to the military's violent and primary function. Femininity is thus constructed in opposition to that of the combatant soldier. This ultimately defines the social being of women in the military. No matter their contribution to the military, their embodiment of femininity means that women are perceived to be excluded from these essentially male and masculine formations. Women's soldiering in the frames of violence and war is a worthy, albeit culturally anomalous, sacrifice.

Equally, military values, ideologies and patterns of behaviour entrench patriarchy. Ideologies of idealised masculinity valorise and epitomise that which is manly, thus creating an iconic male figure. Being a soldier is purposefully linked to being a 'real man'. The values, attitudes, actions, thinking and modes of behaviour that are most appreciated within the military are connected to stereotypical constructions of male and female relations. They are built on a gendered division of labour. The military taps into masculine assets of soldiering by contrasting them with images of femininity.[6] Traditional African gender notions of patriarchy situate women as appendages of men. Women are characterised in relation to their traditional and cultural roles of mothers, sisters, wives and daughters, and therefore viewed as nurturers, carers, homemakers and life givers rather than in reference to their professional abilities and training. While these roles are important in themselves, they are seen as only relevant in relation to the male roles of providers, leaders and decision-makers. Femininity is thus equated with weakness, vulnerability and feebleness.[7]

This article examines 'feminine masculinity' in women's experiences in war and the military through the lens of military combat roles. It explores the interplay of the contradictory dynamics of gender in the military through the lens of Kenyan women combatants in the war against al-Shabaab insurgents in Somalia. It reveals the different gendered characteristics of the military, as reflected in the women's soldierly experiences. The article uses the twin theoretical frameworks of sociocultural capital and cultural scripts, refined by a gender-framing perspective, to interpret the sociocultural attitudes of masculinity and femininity in terms of war, the military and militarism.

Gendered perceptions and integration in the Kenyan military

Women were recruited into the post-colonial Kenya military for the first time in 1972. Prior to this they belonged to a women's only military unit, the Women Service Corps (WSC). It was only after the December 1999 declaration that disbanded the WSC that women were co-opted into the main arms of the Kenya Defence Forces (KDF). Until then, women were prohibited from the majority of roles and operations that require a higher level of physical performance, such as combat and infantry. Women were confined to auxiliary roles and had 'special terms and conditions' that took into account their 'special needs'. Some of these conditions included unwritten policies that women soldiers were not allowed to marry, become pregnant or have children while in service. Many of these discriminatory rules have been removed, giving Kenyan women the space to compete with men in the military. Women and men now serve under the same employment conditions: they are subject to the same selection and training procedures, and no ranks are exclusively reserved for men. They can marry, become pregnant (even when single), and carry out soldierly duties alongside their male counterparts in any of the departments in the Kenyan Army, Air Force and Navy.[8] In addition to the traditional support musters, all frontline musters – such as ground combat, infantry, tank, and commando units – are open to women to compete with their male colleagues.

The integration of women into the military is part of the Kenyan government's action plan to implement United Nations Security Council Resolution (UNSCR) 1325 (2000) on Women, Peace and Security, which commits member states to the increased participation of women in peacekeeping operations and military structures (including civilian police).[9] Further, military recruitment in Kenya is guided by the one-third-gender rule in the constitution,[10] which states that no more than two-thirds of the members of public bodies shall be of the same gender.[11] These principles are founded on the need to see women as key actors and agents for change in society. Despite a substantive increase in the number of women entering into military structures, their inclusion has resulted in an entrenchment, rather than transformation, of sexist ideologies. The military, therefore, remains a highly masculine environment. This has produced ambiguity in terms of how female soldiers are viewed, which is reflected in the evaluation of women's deployment and public reactions to Kenya's military operations in Somalia.

Female combatants and the Kenya Defence Forces' operations in Somalia

National security is the primary concern of any state, and the use of force and militarism are generally accepted as legitimate ways to protect state sovereignty. It is in pursuit of national security that in the last quarter of 2011, the KDF assembled along the border with war-torn Somalia, in preparation for launching assaults on al-Shabaab insurgents. Al-Shabaab was deemed to be behind several kidnappings of foreigners from beach resorts, dealing a major blow to Kenya's tourism industry.[12] One month after the KDF incursion, the Kenyan government agreed to re-hat its forces under the African Union Mission in Somalia (AMISOM) and were later formally integrated after the United Nations Security Council (UNSC) passed Resolution 2036. Christened Operation Linda Nchi (literally translated to mean Operation Protect the Country/State), the KDF assignment initially involved pushing al-Shabaab rebels far inside Somalia, away from the common border. AMISOM's role was to end the Islamist insurgency for good. The KDF, backed by soldiers from the Somali National Army and local anti-al-Shabaab and pro-government militia groups, quickly overran Somalia's southern axis and captured the port city of Kismayo. The city was al-Shabaab's central base and the port was its economic engine, providing an estimated US$35–50 million per year to the group.[13]

The assault on Kismayo was well choreographed. The operation was coordinated, directed, overseen, supervised and undertaken by a contingent of soldiers comprised of women combatants. News of the KDF's overrunning and liberating Kismayo, and other towns and villages across southern Somalia, was soon disseminated.[14] Though Kenyans were initially overjoyed with the successes achieved at the battlefront, the news that female soldiers were at the frontlines of the operation was received with surprise, shock, disbelief and amazement. Lead media stories focused on the surprising, unbelievable and even inappropriate nature of the event.[15] How could the KDF deploy women soldiers to battle al-Shabaab? Many Kenyans could not reconcile the image of the soldier, as a life-taker, with the constructed image of women as peacemakers and life-bearers (mothers, wives, sisters and daughters). In addition, with no effective government, Somalia is one of the world's most dangerous places to operate.

The public reaction to the KDF's 'Somalia operation' raises pertinent questions about the core assumptions of the nature of African femininity and mothering at one level, and masculinity, militarism, soldiering and warfare at another level. For example, what are the sociocultural attitudes about women in the armed forces? Is soldiering incompatible with mothering? How does women's soldiering and ability challenge the very nature of the military and militarism? How does women's soldiering, femininity and ability contribute to strategic military objectives? This study explores the interplay of the contradictory dynamics of gender in the military through the lens of Kenyan women combatants in the war against the al-Shabaab insurgents.

Gender framing, sociocultural capital and cultural scripts

A study of the military and warfare is basically a study of the radical reproduction of traditional gender relations, concepts and division of labour. Lorber describes gender as an

> institution that establishes patterns of expectations for individuals, orders the social processes of everyday life, is built into the major social organizations of society, such as the economy, ideology, the family, and politics, and is also an entity in and of itself.[16]

Scott contends that 'gender is a constitutive element of social relationships based on perceived differences between sexes', and 'is a primary way of signifying relationships of power'.[17] Changes in the organisation of social relationships always correspond to changes in representations of power, but the direction of change is not necessarily one way.

Ridgeway and Correll highlight how gender framing, founded on stereotypical gender rules in society, shapes behaviour and judgements in ways that create systematic patterns of inequalities.[18] These patterns of inequality influence work norms and job matching. Sewell posits that structures are comprised simultaneously of cultural schemas (which are 'key conventions, recipes, scenarios, principles of action and habits of speech and gesture') and resources (which can be human, such as physical strength, knowledge, dexterity and emotional commitment, or nonhuman, such as land and factories).[19]

The military can thus be understood as a structure whose resources (e.g., division of labour) are the effects of schemas (e.g., femininity and masculinity, soldiering and motherhood), just as the schemas are the effects of resources. Within this conceptualisation, the gender structure is both stable and undergoing dynamic changes.

There are two dominant and intersecting cultural schemas in women's enlistment into military combats: the gender schema and the military schema. The gender schema constructs a binary order based on perceived differences between the sexes, and is a primary way of signifying relationships of power. Since the military is culturally defined as masculine, the evaluative bias in favour of men is stronger. The military schema is based on the gender schema. Thus, the military schema creates hierarchies of those who do not fit (physically or emotionally) the imperative of warrior masculinity, those who serve in non-combat roles, and those who resist the warrior ethos altogether. The intersection of the binary gender schema and the military schema shapes the construction of militarised identities, the military's daily practices, social stratification and the link between military service and citizenship.

On the dimension of resources, the military is a male-dominated territory where masculinity is the norm. Women comprise a small percentage of the army and are easily exempted from certain tasks on the grounds of their gender. These structural and organisational differences, together with a patriarchal culture, limit the range of military roles to which women are assigned and constitute a barrier to women's advancement. However, when women are enlisted into combat roles, this gender integration signifies a shift from a gendered structure to a professional-based structure, which may bring about a change in perceptions of femininity and masculinity.

Bourdieu postulates that social actors' chances of succeeding in different fields of action are dependent on the various types of capital – economic, cultural, social and symbolic – that they hold and acquire throughout their lives.[20] The cluster of the different types of capital at any given moment represents the array of obstacles and possibilities in relation to the social action of social groups to which one belongs or wishes to belong. Accordingly, the kinds of capital that women accumulate, the fields of action accessible to them, and their ability to convert the types of capital they hold are different from those among men.

Individuals arrive at the military with different clusters of capital, which are gendered. The military itself creates an assortment of new types of capital. Masculinity and femininity are themselves crucial categories of capital, thereby constructing the meaning of male and female capital and reproducing women's inferiority.[21] This is because 'feminine capital' is the possession of behavioural skills and personal characteristics that accord with the cultural definition of stereotypical femininity.[22]

The concept of cultural scripts stresses the place of social actors in shaping their world. The concept exposes the dynamisms of the ways in which capital is deployed and converted over time; how social agents interpret the cultural script in various social contexts and how actors play with these cultural models, alter them, and replace them.[23] Cultural schemas motivate action and provide templates for socially 'worthy' lives. They are behavioural strategies that offer criteria with which social actors evaluate their current situation and direct their action in the future. As such, they serve as strategies for organising patterns.

The significance of military service in shaping women's life courses is thus tied to the other cultural scripts that are accessible to them (such as seeking fulfilment in being a wife, a mother, a daughter and a sister), and the opportunities that open or close depending on their rank and position. The interplay between the various types of capital acquired or altered during military service and the various cultural scripts shape the meanings women give to military service.

Methodology

This study was carried out between April and August 2014. Data on the military and its activities is highly classified and sensitive. For these reasons, the study used a combination of ethnographic methodologies, including non-participant observation, in-depth conversations, key informant interviews, informal interactions and content analysis. These approaches place the social agent at the centre and are attentive to detailed ethnographies; they therefore allowed a richer, more intimate view of the military vis-à-vis women's experiences than would have been achieved using structured methods. To permit adequate interpretations and analysis, a purposive sample of 10 respondents, including ordinary Kenyan citizens and high-ranking and junior military officers, were recruited for the study. Each sampled population differed in their sense of perceptual and attitudinal adeptness, level of education, training, knowledge, expertise and understanding of the military, its operations, experiences and deployment. The ethnographic data collected was transcribed and analysed – by identifying and coding emerging themes – and then correlated for relationships. The analysed data illustrates the complex and contradictory realities of women in the military.

Feminine soldiering and the warfront

The KDF's 'liberation' of several towns and cities in Somalia inspired pride and patriotism, as well as glorifying combat. Among the KDF soldiers, many women combatants were deployed alongside men in the campaign to dislodge the al-Shabaab militants. The media was awash with images, pictures and articles of female soldiers in martial action, expertly preparing for and participating in combat, drilling proudly in military jungle uniform, carrying weapons, jumping out of warplanes, riding on tanks, and executing amphibian navy attacks.[24] The *Daily Nation* reported that women 'are driving huge rigs down treacherous roads, frisking the militant group al-Shabaab from dangerous dungeons, handling gun turrets, personnel carriers, and providing cover for other soldiers'.[25] The media reports confirmed that female KDF soldiers were serving in soldierly units (pilots, tank drivers, anti-aircraft operators, naval commandos, infantry, armour and field artillery) that 'co-locate' with combat troops.

In confirming the participation of women in the al-Shabaab operation, the KDF spokesperson said: 'Yes, military women are among Kenya's gallant soldiers called on duty to defend the nation from the al-Shabaab. There are women on the frontlines and they are even driving armoured vehicles.'[26] They serve in important roles, including as combatants, clerks, communication technicians, pilots, military police, instructors and lawyers. Others serve as drivers, aircrew, engineers, doctors, nurses, logisticians and air traffic controllers.[27]

Military roles versus feminine roles: perceptions and reality

Many Kenyans wondered if military standards had been lowered to accommodate women in entering combat. Were women subjected to similar standards, similar treatment and similar physical requirements as males? 'We thought women as natural carers are fit for non-combatant tasks such as cooking for and preparing male colleagues for war,' a 40-year-old member of the public noted.[28] 'I have always understood women soldiers to be restricted to prescribed gender roles as nurses, cooks, secretaries and officers in personnel units,' reasoned another 60-year-old member of the public.[29] Another member of the public expressed her misgivings thus:

> I have known women to form part of the defence force of the African traditional societies. In traditional Africa, they were part and parcel of the ferocious warriors that went to war for their people. However, I have never imagined that they would be involved in the modern warfront, doing the actual fighting with the enemy. So women are also trained how to kill? Why should

women be masculinised? I thought their roles remain in supporting male combatants by keeping the supplies alive! Which principle is that, gender equality or what?[30]

Some members of the public, however, borrowed from history and seemed to know and understand that women had been and could be successful warriors. They gave the classic example of Kenya's Mau Mau liberation army, which had many women fighters: 'My grandmother told me that she was a Mau Mau freedom fighter. She even showed me gunshot scars sustained because of her involvement in the freedom struggle. But I sincerely dread the idea of women fighting at the battlefront,' said a 28-year-old woman.[31] In addition, a 50-year-old grandmother fumed:

> Women are fragile objects. We should not allow our women to deadly warfronts like Somalia. I guess we have enough men soldiers to do the battle. Women soldiers can work from the military base but not in the war field.[32]

Nonetheless, in affirming the presence of women in its ranks, the KDF spokesperson said that the highest-ranking woman in the military is a colonel. The KDF spokesperson said Kenya's women in the military are highly disciplined. 'They are as good as the men,' he confirmed.[33] He allayed fears that women are less suited to or qualified for combat:

> Mission success in the military is the number one priority. We want the best and most qualified defending our freedoms and way of life. It doesn't matter if they are pretty, ugly, male, female, tall, or short, as long as they are the best physically, mentally, and emotionally to accomplish the mission of defending our nation. KDF must maintain the most lethal and elite military by meeting a mission standard, not a gender standard. It does not matter if you are a man or a woman. And the mission isn't any less demanding because women accomplish it. Female conscripts have a growing range of duties. Many combat units are dependent on the services of female soldiers.[34]

Military training and patriarchal ideology

Military training is often a tightly choreographed process aimed at breaking down individuality and building official military conduct and group loyalty. This process of socialisation is intimately gendered, as being a soldier is purposefully linked to being a 'real man'. Accounts of training within the KDF show how particular forms of masculinity are cultivated among the troops, which seek to instil courage, control of emotions, willingness to take risks and endure hardships, as well as physical toughness. The ability to suppress fear enables soldiers to engage in combat at great risk to their own safety, while the ability to suppress compassion and empathy enables them to enact violence against others. Shame and humiliation by the use of misogynistic and homophobic slurs are often used to enforce these masculine norms. Masculine ideals of toughness, dominance and heroism are held in high esteem. In answering the question of why patriarchal ideology is a useful element in the making of a soldier, the KDF spokesperson said:

> Military training plays a special role in the ideological creation of soldiers and the notion of combat plays such a central role in the construction of 'manhood'. In the armed forces, there is a deliberate cultivation of masculinity. Trainees are not born soldiers they are made into

soldiers. Becoming a soldier means learning to control fears and domestic longings that are explicitly labelled feminine. Militarists use the myth of war's manliness to define soldierly behaviour and reward soldiers. Trainees are goaded into turning on and grinding down whatever in themselves is 'womanly'. Combat is not just as an important part of being a soldier, it is also an important part of being a man; therefore, to allow women into the central core of the military – combat – is to invite women to the central core of manliness, male identity and thus claims to masculine privilege.[35]

Why do members of the Kenyan public want to see women soldiers in traditional female roles and positions in the military? To fully understand the motivation for this, the KDF spokesperson clarified:

The military is dependent on traditional gender role definitions for its very functioning. The women in the army, in a way, 'raise the morale' of their male colleagues and make the army a home away from home. Thus, as male soldiers leave to fight in combat, female soldiers make it feel as much as possible like a home.[36]

This aspect is more aptly captured by using a family model, as Enloe explains:

'Morale' preoccupies officers, and a good commander is one who can create 'good morale' in the ranks. To portray the soldier's regiment as a 'family' which cares for him and to whom he owes loyalty is one solution. But without women, this is a difficult enterprise. If women can be made to play the role of wives, daughters, mothers, and 'sweethearts', waving their men off to war ... then women can be an invaluable resource to commanders.[37]

Women in the KDF sacrifice social and gender role responsibilities to be able to discharge their soldiery tasks. When asked why she opted to be in the military instead of the comfort of her home, a KDF female sergeant and mother of one said:

I always wanted to join the army. I swore to protect my country and I knew that one day, one time, I would have the opportunity to do what I love and be trained in military college. When you are handed your gun and your ammunition, that means you are prepared. When I joined the military back then, it was hard to imagine this would come to pass but it has and we have to do our job.[38]

Challenging masculinity

It is clear from the foregoing that not only must the numerical domination of men in the military be challenged, but also the ideological foundation of the military as the reproducer of male domination. As women's participation in the military increases, gender stereotyping will decrease. A female captain in the KDF and military survey engineer notes:

If women are to be found bearing arms alongside men, the easy distinction of active warrior men and passive women disappears. A basic distinction between armed men and polite women will no longer be applied. The attribution of effeminacy to all male non-combatants will disappear to apparent logical conclusiveness. Military units will become more representative, and correspondingly, less patriarchal.[39]

A female major in the KDF and air force pilot suggests:

> As long as the military is viewed as the domain of men, women will be outsiders and their participation challenged. Thus, a cycle of male dominance is perpetuated … . This cycle can only be broken if we challenge cultural constructions of sex/gender. Secondly, we should challenge institutional arrangements which allow the perpetuation of distinctions on the basis of sex and gender category. That is, reduce the importance of being feminine or masculine and female or male.[40]

The breaking down of the masculine/feminine gender paradigms will not be accomplished by simply having more women serve in the military; much more needs to be done to change the culture of the military itself.

Military women, technology and warfare

The use of modern-day technological innovations in warfare implies that the military is able to penetrate enemy defences and act with precision, thus reducing the chances of collateral casualties, injury to non-combatant civilians and damage to property. For example, a female captain and military instructor in the KDF registered adeptness with the changing nature of technology in warfare and the tactics involved for its accomplishment in her researched data by outlining the obstacles facing the KDF in Somalia. In her data entitled 'Demography', she points out that, in Somalia, '[l]oyalty revolves around clan' and '[c]lan is a unifying and divisive factor'. Under 'Challenges in Local Areas', she lists 'non-existent government structures' and 'vastness of sector'.[41] Accordingly, the ability of the military to create active offensive operations using, for example, mapping survey information and geospatial systems as its 'weapons' removes the warfront from the fields to the realms of science, research, data and intelligence.

Conclusion

The study draws a conclusion similar to that of Cilliers *et al.*, namely that despite formal policy provisions stipulating that women have an open career path in the military, there still appears to be popular resistance to women serving in combat positions.[42]

Based on an extreme sexual division of labour, women in the military are expected to (re)enact stereotypically feminine behaviours such as nurturing, supporting and being empathetic and caring, while at the same time suppressing these emotions as they face the enemy in combat. They are simultaneously expected to exhibit masculine traits such as bravery, aggression and anger. Thus, the feminised gender role expectations for women are in direct conflict with the masculine warrior culture of the military. Women are called to combine their femininity with the combative masculine stance of the warrior in the military. This puts them slightly apart as colleagues in the military.

Also, as underscored by Juma and Makina, most African countries, Kenya included, are yet to prepare for the full integration of women into their armed forces.[43] They do not have 'operational equipment that is suitable for women. Items as basic as bullet proof vests are not designed for large-breasted women and, in addition, some fighter jet seats do not accommodate large-hipped women'.[44] Adjustments in budget and technology, as well as clearly-defined career paths and equal salaries, are necessary to put women soldiers at the same level as their male colleagues.

With new emphasis on science, research, strategy and electronic technology, the 'front' and 'rear' have receded significantly, with less dependency on physical force and presence in the battle-fields. African nations do not have to continually rely on the physical forms of defence and low technology, which relegate women to being subordinate to men. In conclusion, while military service is a central mechanism for the reproduction of gender relations, for women soldiers it also creates potential spaces for transformation and change.

Acknowledgement

A draft of this manuscript was first presented at the 'Workshop on African Government Forces,' organised by the Nordic Africa institute on the theme: 'New theoretical and methodological approaches,' in Uppsala, Sweden, on 1st and 2nd of December, 2014. I am grateful to the institute for facilitating my participation in the workshop.

Notes

1 H Wright, *Masculinities, conflict and peacebuilding: perspectives on men through a gender lens*, London: Saferworld, 2014; KO Dunivin, Military culture: change and continuity, *Armed Forces & Society*, 20, 1994; J Lorber, From the Editor, *Gender & Society*, 4, 1990.

2 S Faludi, The naked citadel, *The New Yorker*, 5 September 1994; MS Herbert, *Camouflage isn't only for combat: gender, sexuality, and women in the military*, New York, NY: New York University Press, 1998; RC Snyder, *Citizen-soldiers and manly warriors: military service and gender in the civic republican tradition*, Lanham, MD: Rowman & Littlefield, 1999.

3 J Cock, *Colonels and cadres: war and gender in South Africa*, Cape Town: Oxford University Press, 1991; A Mama, Khaki in the family: gender discourses and militarism in Nigeria, *African Studies Review*, 41:2, 1998.

4 L Braudy, *From chivalry to terrorism: war and the changing nature of masculinity*, New York, NY: Vintage, 2005; S Dudink, H Karen, and T Josh (eds.), *Masculinities in politics and war: gendering modern history*, Manchester: Manchester University Press, 2004; C Enloe, *Maneuvers: the international politics of militarizing women's lives*, Berkeley, CA: University of California Press, 2000; PR Higate, 'Soft clerks' and 'hard civvies': pluralizing military masculinities, in PR Higate (ed.), *Military masculinities: identity and the state*, Westport, CT: Praeger, 2003; J Hopton, The state and military masculinity, in PR Higate (ed.), *Military masculinities: identity and the state*, Westport, CT: Praeger, 2003.

5 T Ekiyor, *Female combatants in West Africa: progress or regress?*, Accra: West Africa Network for Peacebuilding, 2002; RS Esuruku, Beyond masculinity: gender, conflict and post-conflict reconstruction in northern Uganda, *Journal of Science and Sustainable Development*, 4, 2011; C Yaliwe, Security sector reform in Africa: a lost opportunity to deconstruct militarised masculinities?, *Feminist Africa*, 10, 2008.

6 C Enloe, *Maneuvers: the international politics of militarizing women's lives*, Berkeley, CA: University of California Press, 2000.

7 T Ekiyor, *Female combatants in West Africa: progress or regress?*, Accra: West Africa Network for Peacebuilding, 2002; RS Esuruku, Beyond masculinity: gender, conflict and post-conflict reconstruction in northern Uganda, *Journal of Science and Sustainable Development*, 4, 2011; C Yaliwe, Security sector reform in Africa: a lost opportunity to deconstruct militarised masculinities?, *Feminist Africa*, 10, 2008.

8 Girl power soars high in military after abolition of Service Corps, *Daily Nation*, 15 December 2013.

9 United Nations Security Council Resolution 1325, S/RES/1325, New York, NY: UN, 2000.

10 Constitution of Kenya, www.kenyaconstitution.org/docs/03cd/005/html, Nairobi: Government of the Republic of Kenya, 2010 (accessed March 2014).

11 M Juma & A Makina, Time for African female soldiers to do more than secretarial work, *Daily Nation*, 4 September 2008; A Smith, *Gender equality? A double standard for women in the military*, 1 May 2014 http://dailycaller.com/2014/01/05/gender-equality-a-double-standard-for-women-in-the-military/

12 Kenyan troops enter Somalia to attack rebels, *Daily Nation*, 16 October 2011.

13 J Verini, KDF breathe new life into Kismayu, *Daily Nation*, 29 December 2012.

14 Ibid.

15 Kenyan troops enter Somalia to attack rebels, *Daily Nation*, 16 October 2011; Who sent our female soldiers to Somalia?, *Daily Nation*, 20 November 2011; P Mathangani, Kenyan women soldiers at the warfront, *Standard Digital News*, 25 October 2011.

16 J Lorber, *Paradoxes of gender*, New Haven, CT: Yale University Press, 1994, 1.

17 JW Scott, *Gender and the politics of history*, New York, NY: Columbia University Press, 1999, 42.

18 C Ridgeway and S Correll, Unpacking the gender system: a theoretical perspective on gender beliefs and social relations, *Gender and Society*, 18, 2011.

19 WH Sewell, A theory of structure: duality, agency, and transformation, *American Journal of Sociology*, 98, 1992, 7.

20 P Bourdieu, The forms of capital, in J Richardson (ed.), *Handbook of theory and research for the sociology of education*, New York, NY: Greenwood Press, 1986.

21 K Huppatz, Reworking Bourdieu's 'capital': feminine and female capitals in the field of paid caring work, *Sociology*, 43, 2009; C Enloe, *Maneuvers: the international politics of militarizing women's lives*, Berkeley, CA: University of California Press, 2000.

22 K Huppatz, Reworking Bourdieu's 'capital': feminine and female capitals in the field of paid caring work, *Sociology*, 43, 2009.

23 SB Ortner, *New Jersey dreaming: capital, culture and the class of '58*, Durham, NC: Duke University Press, 2003.

24 Tough girls take aim at Al-Shabaab militia, *Daily Nation*, 11 November 2011; C Mwaniki, Soldiers showcase skills as they mark KDF day, *Daily Nation*, 14 October 2012.

25 Girl power soars high in military after abolition of Service Corps. *Daily Nation*, 15 December 2013.

26 Interview with KDF spokesperson, 16 April 2014.

27 Tough girls take aim at Al-Shabaab militia, *Daily Nation*, 11 November 2011.

28 Interview with respondent, 6 August 2014.

29 Interview with respondent, 26 July 2014.

30 Interview with respondent, 30 May 2014.

31 Interview with respondent, 30 April 2014.

32 Interview with respondent, 18 June 2014.

33 Interview with KDF spokesperson, 16 April 2014.

34 Ibid.

35 Ibid.

36 Ibid.

37 C Enloe, *Does Khaki Become You? The Militarisation of Women's Lives*, London: Pluto Press Limited, 1983: 5.

38 Interview with KDF respondent, 12 June 2014.

39 Interview with KDF respondent, 10 May 2014.

40 Interview with KDF respondent, 8 July 2014.

41 Interview with KDF respondent, 18 June 2014.

42 J Cilliers et al, Public attitudes regarding women in the security forces and language usage in the SANDF, *African Security Review*, 6:3, 1997.

43 M Juma and A Makina, Time for African female soldiers to do more than secretarial work, *Daily Nation*, 4 September 2008. Available at http://www.nation.co.ke/news/africa/-/1066/467228/-/3j4m49/-/index.html

44 Ibid.

Gender, feminism and food studies

A critical review

Desiree Lewis

Policy research and scholarship on food has rapidly increased in recent decades. The attention to 'gender' within this work appears to signal important practical and academic efforts to mainstream gendered understandings of food consumption, distribution and production into expansive conceptualisations of human security. This article argues that the gender-related work on food has wide-ranging and often troubling political and theoretical foundations and implications. Often growing out of knowledge regimes for managing social crises and advancing neo-liberal solutions, much gender and food security work provides limited interventions into mainstream gender-blind work on the nexus of power struggles, food resources and globalisation. A careful analysis of knowledge production about gender and food is therefore crucial to understanding how and why feminist food studies often transcends and challenges dominant forms of scholarship and research on food security. This article's critical assessment of what food security studies in South Africa has entailed at the regional level and in global terms also focuses on the methodological and theoretical feminist interventions that can stimulate rigorous conceptual, research and practical attention to what has come to be understood as food sovereignty.

Introduction

Policy research, development practice and academic scholarship on food security have mushroomed in recent years. Within this body of research and development practice, work focusing specifically on the gendered dimensions of food systems has also steadily escalated. This article addresses the need to both disaggregate and interrogate the ideological, political, intellectual and, indeed, practical consequences of strands within this work. While this may lay the article open to the charge of 'too much talk about ideas and not enough talk about or for action', I implicitly present a case for thoroughly scrutinising our current industries of development-oriented research and traditions of knowledge, especially when these lay strong claims to engaging pressing social concerns.

Deconstructing which knowledge traditions matter and become dominant and what these traditions yield, as well as which forms of knowledge-making are marginalised and why, is a crucial heuristic practice in an age when much knowledge and information is packaged in rigidly instrumentalist ways. Frequently reduced to 'data' or processed as digestible sound bites, 'knowledge' – disconnected from its roots in political and ideological agendas – is often reconfigured as directly useful information that can be quickly registered, hastily applied, and immediately forgotten. In these circuits of applied information, true socially engaged knowledge and research with the potential to drive long-term and sustainable practice is ultimately jettisoned.

Like human security, food security is a field of research and practice that easily attracts such circuits of information: paradigms and research methods that are galvanised with the aim of urgently responding to social crises, yet which offer very little when scrutinised closely or when applied to the considerable development challenges of marginalised communities or groups. Food security research is therefore an arena where thoughtful attention to the discursive legacies of particular research approaches is especially significant – both in furthering rigorous scholarship and in helping to drive robust socially-engaged practice. This article therefore takes the form of a critical review of the politics of knowledge in the area of food studies and security. It explores trends in global food studies research and food security practice, focusing on their relevance and application to the Global South in general, and South Africa in particular. It also turns to case studies and examples of food security practices to anchor the more general survey-based reflection of scholarship and policy research. My focus is on the Western Cape – the area in which I work and that I know best. As discussed in a subsequent section on methodology, feminist work is invaluably informed by the lived experiences of the researcher-writer, since these both inform and are informed by the situations and subjects that she confronts.

Food security and human security

The centrality of food security to human security has long been on the agenda of international rights instruments, development practice, academic scholarship and policy research. In their report on global patterns of hunger at the start of the new millennium, Louise Fresco and Wilfried Baudoin argued that '[f]ood and nutrition security, besides being a goal in itself, has much larger implications and has to be seen as a contribution to a much broader goal and concept which is improved human well-being and security'.[1] Over a decade ago, Simon Maxwell demonstrated the conceptual and theoretical relevance of establishing the human dimensions of hunger alleviation in a path-breaking article published in the journal *Science Direct*.[2] Yet, in similar ways to human security, exactly *what* 'food security' means, and what it takes to realise this at the local, national and global levels, are matters for which the answers have generally been flattened and simplified.

This is evident in the rapid consolidation of the food security research and policy industry since the middle of the 20th century: in the context of proliferating technologies and discourses of development, the field of food security policy, research and practice has steadily garnered donor support through government funding, North to South aid, United Nations (UN) mechanisms and foreign policy. Alongside this, numerous technologies, university courses, academic projects, policy experts and interdisciplinary paradigms have been harnessed to address the pressing problem of global hunger and 'food insecurity' for the majority of the world's population. A recent Google search of food security institutions yielded 73 300 000 results, with these including non-governmental organisations (NGOs) and non-profit organisations in the Global North and South, summer schools and institutes for training experts and field workers, and a vast body of literature focusing on the problems of the 'food insecure'.

There has been mounting specialisation and sectoral consolidation in these burgeoning areas of agro-food and scientific scholarship and practice. For example, several universities in the Global North now offer specialised graduate programmes. These range from the agro-food focus of the Masters' programme at the Royal Agricultural University in Cirencester, United Kingdom (UK) to the multidisciplinary emphasis at the McGill Institute for Global Food Security in Quebec, Canada. At the same time, there has been a corresponding decline of attention to resources, tools and theories for investigating, understanding and changing social, cultural and historical processes that shape human experiences and subjectivities around food production, consumption and distribution. Interestingly, the Royal Agricultural University unambiguously markets its programmes as career-oriented ones that equip graduates to sell themselves as experts who will apply technical and scientific skills, with very little sociological and historical insight into contexts requiring 'food security' interventions: 'This is the ideal course for those looking for a career in production, policy and sustainable development focusing on food or resource consumption in agriculture ... . This course is particularly appropriate for more mature students who are re-directing their careers.'[3]

It is a predictable irony of our current knowledge economy that a field such as food security studies prioritises productivity, immediate results and short-term solutions, often ignoring the overarching processes (such as environmental degradation, climate change and histories of colonial and neo-colonial appropriation) that led to the world's food crisis existing in the first place. Thus, many within the new field are not familiar with or interested in, for example, the innovative work of the feminist philosopher Nancy Fraser on gender, feminism, social justice and neo-liberalism.[4]

The atomising of the food security research industry (and its severing from scholarship that rigorously investigates power, resource distribution and the historical and discursive construction of dominant knowledge systems) raises the need to do more than simply adding food studies dealing with gender to existing food security work; meaningful interventions would involve investigating the social and political circumstances that led to the emergence and hegemony of the current food security studies industry in the first place. It would also entail addressing the political and interpretive limits of research and policy work in this industry.

One of the research and conceptual gaps resulting from not undertaking this investigation is the absence of work on comprehending and addressing the impact of neo-liberal practice and rhetoric in watering down work that appears to be transformative. And it is noteworthy that neo-liberalism has permeated gendered approaches both to food security and to human security. At the outset, then, a review of how ambiguously gender-related work has responded to mainstream security studies research is necessary. The relationship between mainstream and gendered approaches to food security is very similar to the relationships between gender-blind and gendered approaches to food security: on the one hand, work on gender has invaluably complemented gender-blind discussions of food; on the other, certain traditions of work on gender can easily buttress and assimilate the intentions and thrust of mainstream approaches. Elsewhere, I have described the impact and form of this buttressing and assimilation in South African gender policymaking and planning, arguing that:

> The technicist and instrumentalist approach to gender mainstreaming, achieved by using formulaic skills to establish gender disaggregated data which leads to clearly quantifiable 'outputs' is indebted to the Harvard model-type approach that has come to play a major role in supporting

> neo-liberal development in third-world contexts ... South Africa's gender legislation and policies ... are certainly not mere evidence of patriarchal and elite manipulation. But what does warrant attention is the way a technology of development has come to serve as an overarching framework for thinking about gender in South Africa. This framework, rather than dealing with complex and multi-layered ... social processes, tends to reduce human beings to functional cyphers requiring efficient integration into the modernising and developmental process.[5]

As indicated above, neo-liberalism has had an overarching impact on the language in gendered research on development as well as the vision of transformation embedded in this work. Vigilant and thorough investigation of this work is therefore more than an intellectual or archival exercise; it is part of a vital political intervention into the field of security studies.

In the sections that follow, I tease out various dimensions of this intervention. I explore some of the central concerns within critical work on food and gender politics, drawing particular attention to how these concerns signal the human dimensions of food security and, in substantive ways, establish links between food security and human security. These concerns have been identified by scholars in fields that include cultural studies, critical streams within development studies and interdisciplinary humanities scholarship incorporating history, social geography and gender studies. Much of this work has not, however, been consolidated as a distinct field; nor has its epistemological import been clearly identified vis-à-vis existing regimes of knowledge about food, social justice, and individuals' and groups' security and well-being. The primary aim of this article is to address these overarching concerns.

Discursive space-clearing

As the 'primary cognitive lens through which the complexity and prevalence of global hunger is viewed',[6] food security can be investigated as a technology of governance institutionalised by the UN and, more broadly, the agendas of corporate global capitalism. From this perspective, 'food security' is not a self-evident linguistic term that 'captures' objectively measurable social and human experiences; rather, it actively constitutes our understanding of such experiences. Consequently, in similar ways to phrases such as 'public participation', 'sustainable development', 'gender transformation', and other current terms in neo-liberal 'public good' discourses (and much academic, social policy research), it conjures up a sense of urgency to legitimise the marshalling of specialised actions, material resources, vocabularies, skills and institutions to address social problems. At the same time, like these phrases, it is often either lifted out of, or discursively constructed against, particular historical, cultural and epistemological frameworks. In this way it is presented as a neutral and self-evident area of social intervention that requires urgent and focused remedies.

Compelling arguments are usually made for the need for this positivist approach: real problems, the argument goes, need specialised concepts and urgent, focused problem-solving. And anti-positivist analysis of culture, history and discourse/text in the face of the urgent problems they claim to lay bare is deemed to be gratuitous, self-indulgent or socially irrelevant – hence the proliferation of funding for particular market-driven and developmentalist-oriented subjects and fields in the Global South. In South Africa, for example, the Western Cape provincial government provides food security grants to 'support only groups from the historically disadvantaged communities who want to start a garden'.[7] Government rhetoric further stresses that, 'The Department of

Agriculture will give financial assistance to 20 groups each year for the next three years to support the Food Security Drive ... . This programme wants to support especially women and youth groups.'[8]

On the one hand, the professed commitment to the food security needs of poor women and young people is – at face value – laudable; on the other hand, the Western Cape provincial government, like the national government, has been notably restrained about the long-term socio-economic needs of communities in South Africa through, for example, health care, service delivery, employment, higher wages for workers, and housing; all these would be central to their food security. The situation in the Western Cape is not dissimilar to that in many other contexts in the Global South, where funding and grants provided by international donors and governments are made available with the professed aim of alleviating food security, although there is very limited attention to the structural causes of that insecurity. To a large extent, then, food security funding and grants act as quick fix panaceas – provided in lieu of substantial financial support for and political commitment to the broad security needs of poor and struggling communities.

As Heidi Hudson has shown, feminist work on social justice and human security can play a significant role in establishing more inclusive bottom-up approaches that are sensitive to the structural causes of insecurity.[9] This is because much of the work on gender, feminism and human security seeks to interrupt dominant bodies of knowledge that simplify questions about and answers to what threatens the well-being of gendered, raced and classed social subject human beings at the micro, macro and global levels. In so doing, it raises epistemological ideas about whose knowledge matters, the perspectives from which knowledge about human security is produced, and how certain voices may be drowned out in canonical and hegemonic perspectives of academic studies, policy research and human rights discourse. Hudson writes:

> Machismo, heralded by the post-9/11 global war against terror, threatens to drown out the progress made during the 1990s with regard to building a global normative consensus on the importance of human security. Today, more than ever, human security coexists uneasily with national security. Since the analytical potential of feminist epistemology cannot be divorced from its political and transformative value, a critical feminist perspective on the study of security, and especially human security, is crucial to overcome certain gender silences. ... feminism refers to the area where theory and practice meet with regard to transforming the unequal power relationships between women and men. It is more than an intellectual enterprise for the creation of knowledge. It also draws on the struggles of the women's movement and the theorizing emanating from those experiences.[10]

Similar interruptions, which squarely foreground gender or take feminism into account, have characterised the fields of food security and sovereignty. Within the broad field of gender and food security, research varies theoretically, and scholars have come up with wide-ranging recommendations. These include addressing government policies and development practice,[11] instituting women's small-scale and community-driven empowerment projects and critiquing multiple power dynamics in explaining how and why particular gendered groups bear the worst brunt of food inequalities.[12] It is noteworthy that these interpretations focus mainly on how and why certain groups are marginalised or victimised. The consequence of this is an emphasis on how to assist, develop or support subordinated groups, especially women, with tools, resources and expertise external to their own local knowledge economies, food technologies and food systems.

At the margins of this research on gender and food are feminist studies of food sovereignty, which seek to do much more than identify the victims of food inequalities. Exploring food sovereignty, whether in practice or through research, has meant addressing relations of power and control around rights to food, the role of markets and governments, corporate agriculture and Big Food oligarchies. The Food Sovereignty Campaign in South Africa is an important example. As a new alliance, the campaign is committed to forging solidarity among organisations that deal with landlessness, exploitation and injustice. During its assembly at the start of 2015, several organisations representing the hungry, the landless and the exploited pledged themselves to concerted action to transform existing food systems and their origins in injustice and exploitation. The campaign's declaration is unequivocal about a holistic approach to social justice and transformation:

> We came together at the Assembly through our shared understanding that we have a crisis-ridden corporate and globalised food system that is responsible for worsening social, health and climate challenges, and which is coinciding with increasing state failure in relation to regulating our food regime and ensuring much needed agrarian transformation. Such a struggle-driven national Food Sovereignty Campaign is unprecedented in the context of South Africa and has drawn inspiration from local food sovereignty practices and from the rising international movements and alliances championing food sovereignty in different parts of the world … . We are not simply calling for technical solutions for households to access food as encapsulated in the government's recently proposed Food Security and Nutrition Policy and Implementation Plan. We reject the latter and instead are calling for the deep transformation of our food system by breaking the control of food corporations, repositioning the state to realise the Constitutional right to food and as part of creating the conditions and space for the emergence of food sovereignty alternatives from below.[13]

This attention to struggles related to power relations shifts the focus away from ideas about increased food production or availability that often characterises food security research and interventions. Explaining this by invoking La Via Campesina, who pioneered the concept of food sovereignty, Raj Patel writes:

> Just like the definition of food security, food sovereignty is an evolving and multi-faceted term, but it has an invariant core: 'communities have the right to define their own food and agriculture policy'. To be clear, sovereignty is not a call for self-sufficiency, for states to grow within their borders sufficient food to feed their citizens. La Via Campesina instead calls for people to be sovereign over their food systems, for people to have the power to decide what the system should look like. This is an intentionally vague call, with many questions left open-ended, so that the communities involved in claiming food sovereignty might answer issues around production, distribution, and consumption of food for themselves.[14]

In particular, food sovereignty research focuses on marginalised groups' active struggles and agencies in resisting hunger, rising food crises, food marketing monopolies and the like.

Illustrating how feminism questions consensual ideas about objective or neutral knowledge, this work demonstrates that particular bodies of knowledge in academia, policy research, development practice and the public domain acquire a sense of neutrality and authority because of their hegemony. It is therefore unsurprising that gender and food security work has marshalled considerable support from governments, international donors and Northern governments. Feminist scholarship on food encourages us to think about how much of our commonsensical and positivist information and knowledge about food, hunger and hunger alleviation are discursively constituted.

While feminist constructionists are of course not the only scholars who do this, feminist attention to standpoint epistemologies has alerted us to how the givens of our world are defined by the vantage points of those who do the defining.[15] Given the authority of positivist food security discourses, industries and technologies, feminist deconstructions offer tools, theoretical frameworks, methodologies and epistemological critiques for a kind of discursive space clearing around how we talk about food. It can allow us to take a step back away from many positivist and straightforward assumptions about food resources, hunger and power, and develop what Patel describes as a 'heuristic approach to power' and 'a means not only to interpret the system, but also to change it'.[16]

Indigenous knowledge systems and voices from below

One consequence of this discursive space clearing is to create space for voices that are usually drowned out by research and policy experts on global food crises. These marginalised perspectives have often been described in terms of the category of 'indigenous knowledge systems' (IKS) – but it is worth reflecting critically on how these systems have been yoked to dominant food discourses that shut down on much more than they open up. It has been noted by several researchers that IKS within the global knowledge economy are important areas of intervention, since they embed the values, visions and strategies that groups have developed over several generations.[17] Such knowledge systems therefore disrupt the hegemony of capitalist, state-driven, elite and often patriarchal knowledge, all of which enjoy tremendous authority as 'expertise' or 'science' in the face of 'tradition'. The attention to IKS in sub-Saharan Africa has been particularly significant, and is often defined as a valuable source for energising developmental processes in society that are not driven from above. Interestingly, a World Bank definition of IKS in sub-Saharan Africa notes that:

> Indigenous knowledge is part of the lives of the rural poor; their livelihood depends almost entirely on specific skills and knowledge essential for their survival. Accordingly, for the development process, indigenous knowledge is of particular relevance for the following sectors and strategies: agriculture; animal husbandry and ethnic veterinary medicine; use and management of natural resources.[18]

One problem with the field of IKS is the tendency to dwell on rural contexts and agriculture as though these are the only terrains in which alternative marginalised voices talk back to dominant food distribution, sale and growth patterns. Much of the work on IKS, food and gender focuses on African rural women subsistence farmers and their indigenous agricultural knowledge. The aim is therefore to mainstream this knowledge or ensure that it is taken into account in policymaking and agricultural planning – and the implicit assumption is that alternatives can come only through what is authentically rural and agricultural. While agriculture and rural contexts are important, the emphasis on these contexts and neglect of others is disturbing. IKS is therefore seen as being in danger of becoming extinct, with the challenge of 'salvaging' threatened knowledge becoming a priority.

As several scholars have shown, Southern Africa – as is the case with many other parts of Africa – is characterised by rapid urbanisation, with many of the squatter camps, informal settlements and townships mushrooming as immigrants from rural areas and beyond the borders of individual

countries settle in and beyond city centres.[19] The especially swift growth of peri-urban areas is tes-
timony to the hybridisation of geographical spaces, subjectivities and lifestyles, with poor, unemployed people being unable to 'live off the land' and remaining wholly dependent on supermarkets,
small traders and corner shops for their food needs. The notion of 'indigenous' knowledge systems
does not quite do justice to the hybridised, inventive and extremely dynamic negotiations that
certain subjects perform in empowering themselves vis-à-vis global food corporations, rising
food prices, Big Food operations and rampant liberal economics that absolve governments of
responsibility for their citizens' food needs. Moreover, the belief that individuals in these circumstances experience uniform victimisation is a gross simplification of poor consumers' agencies and
resources for resistance. For example, work in the informal food sale sector shows that many are
able to sell and buy food at reduced prices or on credit, and this makes them less vulnerable to
Big Food and the high food prices of supermarkets and fast food chains.

IKS studies on food also suffer from a tendency to see indigenous knowledge as sealed off
domains that exist in isolation from modernity and external imperialist-capitalist influence.
More useful than this reductive way of thinking about embattled indigenous knowledge is to
explore knowledge-making about food consumption, distribution and growth as dynamic, even
though marginalised, subaltern and gendered. In other words, these peripheral traditions of
knowing can be thought about as oppositional and dynamic bodies of knowledge that contest
changing local patriarchal authorities, elite-driven economic policies and practices, and global com-
modity capitalism. Exploring and analysing local bodies of knowledge, especially those developed
by women, would allow us to understand the complex livelihoods and food acquisition strategies
that certain groups and individuals develop – despite their apparent entrapment in deprivation and
poverty. As some of the work on IKS has shown, it would also counter the top-down emphasis in
the specialist field of food security. For example, taking into account what particular groups know
about nutrition and well-being in relation to certain plants and foodstuffs means engaging with
long-established understandings of how human beings have confronted their local environment,
and available routes for obtaining and producing nourishing food.

Equally importantly, it would consider the central role of food in systems of organisation and
rituals where central, often pivotal social values are celebrated, confirmed and defended. A valuable
insight into this is Anna Madoeuf's study of feasts in Cairo, Egypt. Madoeuf describes the vibrancy
and richness of the *moulid* as a central food event that combines religious celebration, carnival and
feasting among Cairo's city dwellers. Especially notable is the writer's attention to how this food
event cements relationships, in particular urban spaces, thus involving Egyptians' encounters
with food in ways that far exceed the simple processes of consumption and nutrition. Madoeuf
therefore demonstrates that food studies should be integral to understanding the complex ways
in which human beings establish relationships to and through food.[20]

Exploring the South African context, and the Western Cape in particular, Gabeba Baderoon
draws similar conclusions in her study of food and cooking among Muslims. On the one hand,
she critically analyses the way Muslim people's cuisine has been 'exoticised' as 'Malay' cooking
through discursive practices that erase Muslims' actual experiences of food and confirm racist
constructs of the benign, exotic and tractable 'Cape Malay'. On the other hand, Baderoon
shows how Muslim women who began writing and publishing their own cookbooks inter-
rupted traditions of exoticised 'Malay' food cultures. Muslim women who wrote their own
cookbooks therefore testified not only to their own knowledge of particular recipes, but also
to the rich, complex subjectivities and cultural processes associated with particular food
events and recipes.[21]

Apart from the insight provided into certain groups' own knowledge of food, national cuisine and nutrition, understanding local bodies of knowledge about food would provide crucial avenues into understanding food flows as sites of resistance and socially marginalised groups' agencies. Many marginalised and exploited women have devised inventive ways of resisting exploitative food chains and procured, produced or prepared cost-effective and nutritious foods for themselves and others. Examining how organisations or even small support groups negotiate women's empowerment in relation to rising food process and market monopolies is crucial to any feminist effort to explore food sovereignty, and to correct the emphasis on victimisation in much food security studies. The Western Cape's significant tradition of these organisations in the form of the Surplus People Project and Women on Farms could stimulate important work by feminists who engage carefully with and listen to the voices of local women who are forging their own solutions and survival strategies in the face of food insecurity.

A valuable example of an organisation that has addressed not only groups' bottom-up approaches to food security but also the complex psychological and emotional repercussions of food struggles is the Gender Equity Unit at the University of the Western Cape. Having emerged in the wake of efforts to pursue gender and other forms of justice on campus during the early 1990s, the unit has run a food programme for hungry students on campus for several years. Unlike welfarist food donation projects, however, this unit tries to connect the eradication of hunger to the acquisition of dignity and the instilling of a collective consciousness of injustice and responsibility. The aim of the project is therefore to build awareness around attitudes towards hunger and poverty rather than simply position hungry students as being in need of rescue. The objective is to encourage a sense of collective accountability among the entire campus community, rather than to single out 'hungry students' as a problem to be mechanically fixed and as the object of others' 'generosity'.

This programme has always seemed to me an extremely politically valuable one, not only because of its attention to power but also because of its nuanced attention to the cultural and psychological meanings of hunger and poverty. In illustrating a food sovereignty approach, the project foregrounds the social and psychological dimensions of hunger and poverty as dimensions that are often rendered invisible in many conventional food security approaches. Amartya Sen has been influential in encouraging us to link poverty to 'shame', and therefore understand fully what hunger means to people as human beings.[22] In distinguishing between capabilities and functioning, he argues that the facilities enabling human beings to realise their capabilities are shaped by cultural factors and access to resources.[23] In the same way that Sen identified 'the ability to go about without shame' as a capability at the 'irreducible absolutist core in the idea of poverty', shame can also be linked to hunger, generating syndromes of helplessness and inadequacy around the inability to provide or participate.[24]

The more pragmatic approaches to food insecurity neglect these complex factors, ignoring ways in which the perceptions, voices and feelings of marginalised groups are pivotal to strategies for their empowerment and security as human beings. Using a feminist standpoint approach to take into account marginalised voices and bodies of knowledge would therefore mean not only understanding the ways in which subordinated subjects actively respond to challenges, or develop their own strategies for growing, procuring or distributing food; it would also mean understanding their feelings about what it means to be hungry and, therefore, what measures – whether local or broader – best succeed in their struggles for full empowerment.

The advocacy and critical literacy work pursued by the Gender Equity Unit shows a deep understanding of how hunger affects embodied and culturally-determined subjects, and how the eradication of hunger needs to be connected to understanding its cultural, emotional and psychological dimensions. Such practical work therefore embeds valuable knowledge-making. An emphasis on behavioural responses to food could go a long way towards understanding the intricacies of food consumption and distribution among both the 'stuffed and the starved', as Patel puts it, instead of the usual fixation only on the starving, as though food crises today are simply a matter of making sure that the hungry are fed, and not the fact that the current global capitalist monopolising, sale and marketing of food creates a food crisis for us all.[25]

Intersectionality, interdisciplinarity and food studies

Work on gender is sometimes understood to entail the identification and analysis of gender (and sometimes even of women) as a neatly identifiable unit of study that can be factored into or exist alongside traditional work that ignores gendered relations and powers. But central to feminist intellectual and political work since the late 1900s is the understanding that gender is always related to other social identities. Thus, intersectionality (the entanglement of multiple identities in everyday struggles and broad global processes) or, in more recent theorising, 'assemblage', has become the focus of inquiry of current feminist work.

Taking intersectionality into account also means fully embracing interdisciplinarity. One of the disturbing features of certain food security studies is that they are locked into highly sectoralised zones of expert knowledge. As the preceding discussion of aspects of applied research as well as sites of graduate study at universities indicates, the recent industry of food security studies has spawned several domains of expert knowledge, often driven by the North, by elites and by scholars who work in tandem with the agendas, and even the directives, of governments and donors. These domains are often marked by blunt quantitative methods and positivist approaches that manage more than they explain. A revealing example is a study of food insecurity in Limpopo, one of the poorest provinces in South Africa, undertaken by a consortium comprising the universities of Stellenbosch, Pretoria, Ghent and Antwerp, and the South African government's Department of Agriculture. The report growing out of this project is revealing about blunt positivistic methods used to generate mainly quantitative data about salient problems, such as how women and children are most affected by food scarcity in poor rural communities.[26]

The report is also indicative of the way in which tremendous resources and efforts are invested in generating statistics through, for example, the administering of questionnaires or organisation of focus groups, methodologies that often limit researchers' insights into how their respondents complicatedly engage with food crises. Lastly, the project and report are revealing about particular alliances and collaborations among academic and state sources that generate flows of funding, knowledge-making and cooperation for experts and elites, while the poor and starving remain objects or beneficiaries of expert knowledge.

In contrast to such studies, the kind of interdisciplinary research that feminists have always undertaken draws eclectically on various disciplines to transcend this arrogant production of knowledge in silos. A fairly recent example of this work is a special issue of the journal *Feminist Africa*, 'Land, labour and gendered livelihoods', which seeks to draw together the usually separated areas of land, labour and livelihoods.[27] Focusing on ways in which cross-disciplinarity can sharpen theoretical and conceptual frameworks for dealing with the micro and macro levels, contributions carefully engage with gendered, domestic, communal and national levels, showing how access to and control over land and resources is vitally connected to patterns of formal, informal and invisibilised labour, as well as to the ways in which particular groups and social subjects secure and struggle for livelihoods.

As contributions to this special issue reveal, one of the many consequences of embracing intersectionality is to recognise food as a site of struggle and so contribute to expanding theorists' attention to food sovereignty, rather than to food security. Carolyn Sachs' 'Feminist food sovereignty: crafting a new vision' shows that recent interdisciplinary feminist food studies confront – at the local and wider levels – constant struggles over the control and access to resources and around the representation and ascription of identities.[28] Such struggles are multifaceted and include certain middle-class food consumers' efforts to eat well, women farmers' resistance to corporate monopolisation, individual or collective efforts to control the representation and definition of 'eating well', individuals' gendered resistance to food in the form of anorexia or bulimia, and individual or group representations of 'good food', 'cooking' and cuisine in struggles for individual prestige or cultural or social autonomy. Such social, individual and creative struggles should be crucial to an analysis that avoids stereotyping 'victims' in current food systems. These also connect communal and regional struggles over hunger to broader struggles and systems of meaning making.

Interdisciplinary work on gender and food encourages us to make connections between the materialities of food and discourses around food and eating. Exploring the human dimensions of social, economic and political processes around food therefore offers a place for cultural studies approaches. These can uncover connections between the social and political practices around food and ideologies of food and eating. In their discussion of 'visceral politics', the authors of the journal article 'Taking back taste: feminism, food and the visceral politics' illustrate the value of these humanities approaches by considering how social subjects' beliefs are linked to their everyday experiences of food.[29] Drawing on post-structural feminism, they unravel plays of power in and around food, tracing power through the body in order to understand the making of the political (eating) subject. Such understanding is not done in the interests of theoretical or analytical dexterity; rather, analysing beliefs, representation and meanings associated with food, eating and the body 'is crucial to the ability of food-based movements to inspire action across difference and achieve their progressive goals'.[30]

Overall then, interdisciplinary feminist approaches to food amplify understandings of power, resistance and freedoms in particular contexts. While the pressing problems of hunger and deprivation have understandably led to a fixation with those who are obviously starving, both hunger and overeating are – as Patel cogently observes – symptoms of a single system.[31] Who eats or overeats and the conditions under which they eat, as well as who is deprived and what social criteria we use to measure this deprivation, warrant scrutiny not only of obviously visible power relations but also of hidden influences. Such coercive influences could be manifested in anorexia and excessive dieting or obesity as a result of fast food consumption among the poor in developed countries. Encompassing mass media texts, advertising and even so-called scientific and public health messages, these influences echo dominant discourses of gender, class, imperialism and capitalism in local and global social imaginaries.

It is worth stressing how important humanities work is to this interdisciplinary work on food. Among others, Stephen Arnold has dealt critically with the marginalisation of the humanities in development studies, describing it as the brittle nature of development studies, in which 'humans are treated as cyphers and problems become abstractions requiring technical solutions'.[32] Fiction is often an extremely valuable source of knowledge about the politics of food and hunger;

in fact, in similar ways to many feminist studies, fiction frequently explores the cultural and meta-phoric complexities and cultural relativity of 'hunger', food and eating. In Anita Desai's novel, *Fasting, feasting*, the dislocation and alienation of an Indian immigrant in the United States (US) is explored in relation to his struggles to eat well (on his terms), while the daughter of the American family with whom he lives overeats compulsively as she experiences her own painful sense of alien-ation and body dysmorphic disorder in a world obsessed with conspicuous consumption alongside obsessions around body image.[33] The novel intricately unravels the contradictory and multiple layers of distress, discomfort and deprivation associated with food consumption and acquisition in North–South dynamics, exploring ways in which class, region, gender and race are intricately webbed in the meanings attached to and the circuits of food. As a work of fiction, Desai's insight is distinctive in dwelling on character and consciousness in ways which scholarship simply cannot. At the same time, it is worth stressing that much feminist work, because of its efforts to challenge linear and masculinist content and forms of knowledge, is acutely alert to the kinds of intersections around power that Desai's novel explores.

Methodological innovations

Attentiveness to indigenous and marginalised bodies of food knowledge is connected to a crucial area for feminist interventions into food and human security studies; namely, the value of policy or scholarly research that effectively identifies and 'hears' knowledge-making beyond academia – i.e., knowledge-making among marginal groups. Much feminist research has been path-breaking in developing methodological approaches that unsettle conventional researcher-researched relations and therefore uncover more expansive sources and forms of knowledge. Some of the most demo-cratising methodological work in the social sciences and humanities has emanated from feminist research and teaching on gender. Such work has entailed, for example, the use of personal narra-tive; participatory action research; genre-blending in research products through incorporating life narratives into scholarship or policy research; and using visual methodologies that encourage a richer and more polysemous analysis than is often the case with written text.

An important example of one such study is Goolam Vahed and Thembisa Waetjen's social history, which uses cookbooks, cultural activities, social circles and networks organised by women in Durban to provide a textured history from below, along with theoretically-focused insight into matters of race, class, caste and gender that are often erased in more orthodox historical studies.[34] It is noteworthy that sections of the study that deal with women's preparation of food, their collection of recipes, the social networks they formed around food rituals, and their authority in feasts and meals within their families and communities are the richest entry points in the authors' analysis of the many-layered private and social experiences of their subjects.

But most importantly, much feminist research is deeply committed to researchers' auto-reflex-ivity as a guiding principle for ensuring the researcher's humility in the face of her subject matter and research participants. In other words, encouraging the researcher to position herself, her own investment in her work, and her inevitably blinkered ways of knowing, in all stages of the research process. It is sometimes striking how often the charge of 'bias' or 'lack of scientific rigour' creeps into the arguments of scholars and students of human security and food security. The assumption is that perspective and standpoint can somehow be eliminated, as though they are faults to be over-come with 'properly scientific measures in other words, the belief that the aim of research is to arrive at universal truths.

As feminists have long shown, claims of scientific rigour or universality are often invoked to mask (inevitably) positioned ways of understanding and knowing. The more challenging task of research is to make transparent these positioned ways of knowing and so uncover more inclusive bodies of knowledge and conversations around these. Feminists who have adopted standpoint epistemologies have therefore argued that it is often through the perspectives of women and other socially subordinate groups that far richer and more productive insights into power relations have emerged. Among these, Patricia Hill Collins and Sandra Harding have provided central responses. As a feminist philosopher of science, Harding contests the naturalised claim to universality in dominant knowledge-making by arguing that, paradoxically, richer political and theoretical ideas are likely to be provided by those at the margins. She writes: 'Starting off research from women's lives will generate less partial and less distorted accounts not only of women's lives but also of men's lives and of the whole social order.'[35] Echoing this in her discussion of black feminist standpoint, Hill Collins insists that black women, like other multiply marginalised groups, are able to develop epistemologies on the basis of their vantage points. These gesture towards universal insights into the 'human', understandings of power and the locations of dominant groups from the perspective of 'seeing from below'.[36]

As discussed above, the field of food security, including the small but growing field of gender and food security, has been marked by rigid and top-down research methods. Often defined as incontrovertible 'science', these can seriously distort and neglect understandings not only of poor and socially marginalised people's experiences of food; they can also distort understanding of the wider food systems in which particular experiences of hunger and powerlessness exist.

One especially promising feminist intervention would involve methodologies linked to the use of visual texts. Several methodologies for using visual texts in mainstream food security studies are already being utilised in food security studies. One participatory action research method, frequently used for developmental projects in South African contexts, is photovoice. As a bottom-up methodology, photovoice uses the registers, images and perspectives of research participants to develop knowledge about particular subjects, and so refuses the idea of research subjects being passive repositories of information. As one study indicates, photovoice can yield important insights into ways in which groups living with HIV/AIDS experience and respond to contextually-specific food and nutritional imperatives, given specific economic, health and health-care constraints.[37] Their work therefore demonstrates how photovoice can support qualitative studies for producing a rich analysis of nutritional security and health, and for providing valuable information in critical public health programmes.

Yet there is much more that visual texts can unravel about food, food cultures and human subjectivities from a feminist perspective. Here I would like to outline some avenues offered by feminist documentary filmmaking, and, in particular, the work of the Cape Town-based film-maker Shelley Barry. Interestingly, Barry's films are not primarily about food; nor do they foreground food as a central theme in the way that they centralise the struggles for dignity of disabled people in mainstream society, or lesbian agencies and black women's experiences. Yet food repeatedly surfaces as a language in Barry's films, providing tropes, images and filters through which the filmmaker explores a host of stories about belonging, sexuality, fulfilment and freedom.

This is especially pronounced in her documentary on the activist writer, Charlene Maslamoney, who died in 2013 after battling cancer for several years. *I'm Not Done Yet* (2014) tells a powerful story about Maslamoney's efforts to heal herself and to help others heal themselves from nutritional, political and spiritual points of view.[38] The story of her final years is interwoven with her encounters and experiments with good food and healthy eating. As an activist, Maslamoney criticises the exorbitant prices of health foods but also confirms the value of eating well, learning to understand the value of certain foods, spices and herbs as well as the desirability of women with limited financial resources doing so. In view of the widespread tendency in public health discourses to pathologise black women as health risks because of their ignorance,[39] the film is a powerful black feminist response that testifies to black women's knowledge and understanding of food. The documentary is a powerful counter to dominant public health didacticism, and the viewer is able to learn crucial lessons about healthy eating by empathetically engaging with the intensely personalised journey of the protagonist as she playfully talks about her spiritual, health and political struggles. It is a film that has clear practical relevance in South Africa, where diseases linked to nutritional security, such as TB, cancer and HIV/AIDS, place many women under particular pressure to eat well in the face of limited economic resources, support networks or health care services. At the same time, it is not a film that dogmatically instructs viewers; rather, it is a form of knowledge-making through visual storytelling that allows the viewer to actively engage with the lessons traced in the protagonist's story.

There is considerable scope for developing the small tradition of feminist as opposed to gender-sensitive research methodologies that actively work with, rather than for, subordinate groups. As Lisa Weasel puts it in her study of India:

> Research in the natural sciences has tended to focus uncritically on technoscientific solutions to the problem of global food security. Yet the intended recipients … often lower-caste women, have in some cases been vehement opponents of these solutions. Qualitative participatory approaches informed by feminist principles, can elucidate the reasons for this rejection and help to chart a more appropriate epistemological orientation for developing solutions based in community members' lives and needs.[40]

Conclusion

In Charles Dickens' famous novel, *Oliver Twist*, the central character pleads: 'Please sir, I want some more.' Set in Victorian England, where capitalist production has begun to entrench divides between the controllers of food resources and the producers who have limited control over these, the novel powerfully illustrates the plight of the 'food insecure'. It also captures the remarkable complacency of the dominant classes. Mr Bumble's outraged response to Oliver's request for more food vividly reveals the refusal of those in positions of relative power to acknowledge the plight of the starving majority. It also powerfully reveals the elite's refusal to hear the masses' voices. In our current context of global capitalist production, the refusal to 'see' starvation or the voices of the hungry seems to be replicated in responses ranging from denial to quick-fix efforts to alleviate deeply embedded economic, political and social circumstances. Unless our responses seek to address these multifaceted circumstances, they will continue to remain part of the problem, rather than a means toward discovering solutions.

Acknowledgements

I am indebted to the Mellon Foundation for funding the project of which my research is part: "Food Politics and Cultures: Humanities Approaches to Food and Food Systems". Begun in June 1015, this project is housed in the Women's and Gender Studies Department at the University of the Western Cape, and is located within the Centre of Excellence on Food Security at UWC.

Notes

1 LA Fresco and W Baudoin, Food and nutrition security towards human security, 2007 www.fao.org/ag/agp/agpc/doc/reports/icv02e90spe.pdf (accessed August 2015), 15.

2 S Maxwell, Food security: a post-modern perspective, *Science Direct*, 21, 1996.

3 Royal Agricultural University, MSc Sustainable Agriculture and Food Security, www.rau.ac.uk/study/postgraduate-study/sustainable-agriculture-and-food-security/sustainable-agriculture-and-food-security-msc

4 N Fraser, Feminism, capitalism and the cunning of history, *New Left Review*, 56, March/April 2009.

5 D Lewis, The politics of 'do-ing gender' in South Africa: implications for social work, *Social Worker Practitioner-Researcher*, 24, 2012, 16.

6 R Alcock, Speaking food: a discourse analytic study of food security, 2009, www.bristol.ac.uk/media-library/sites/spais/migrated/documents/alcock0709.pdf (accessed July 2015) ii.

7 Western Cape Government, Funding and Support, www.westerncape.gov.za

8 Ibid.

9 H Hudson, A feminist perspective on human security in Africa, in H Solomon & M van Aardt (eds.), *'Caring' security in Africa*, Pretoria: Institute for Security Studies, 1998.

10 H Hudson, 'Doing' security as though humans matter: a feminist perspective on gender and the politics of human security, *Security Dialogue*, 36, 2005, 155–156.

11 See M de Klerk et al, Food security in South Africa: key policy issues for the medium term, 2004, http://sarpn.org/documents/d0000685/Food_security_SA_January2004.pdf (accessed July 2015).

12 Institute of Development Studies, Gender and food security: towards gender – just food and nutrition security, 2014, http://opendocs.ids.ac.uk/opendocs/bitstream/handle/123456789/5245/IDS_Bridge_Food_Security_Report_Online.pdf?sequence=3 (accessed July 2015).

13 Food Sovereignty Campaign Coordination Committee, Declaration of the South African Food Sovereignty Campaign and Alliance, 2015, www.copac.org.za/files/Food%20Sovereignty%20Assembly%20Declaration.pdf (accessed August 2015), 1.

14 R Patel, Food sovereignty: power, gender, and the right to food, *PLoS Med* 9(6): e1001223, 1.

15 S Harding, Rethinking Standpoint Epistemology: What is Strong Objectivity?, in L Alcoff & E Potter (eds.), *Feminist Epistemologies*, New York/London: Routledge, 1993.

16 R Patel, Food sovereignty: power, gender, and the right to food, *PLoS Med* 9(6): e1001223.

17 P Bates et al (eds.), *Learning and knowing in indigenous societies today*, Paris: UNESCO, 2009, 3.

18 World Bank, Regions: sub-Saharan Africa, www.worldbank.org/afr/ik/basic.htm (accessed August 2015).

19 A Simone & A Abouhani (eds.), *Urban Africa: changing contours of survival in the city*, Dakar: Codesria Books, 2005.

20 A Madoeuf, *Feasts: panoramas in town – the spaces and times of the moulids of Cairo*, Pretoria: Codesria, 2005.

21 G Baderoon, *Regarding Muslims*, Johannesburg: Wits University Press, 2014.

22 A Sen, *Commodities and capabilities*, Oxford: Oxford University Press, 1985.

23 A Sen, Poor, relatively speaking, *Oxford Economic Papers*, 35, 1983.

24 Ibid., 165.

25 R Patel, Food sovereignty: power, gender, and the right to food, *PLoS Med* 9(6): e1001223.

26 National Agricultural Marketing Council, Food security vulnerability in South Africa: case study Limpopo, www.namc.co.za/upload/presentation/Presentation%20food%20security%20limpopo%20final1.pdf (accessed July 2015).

27 F Liersch (ed.), *Land, labour and gendered livelihoods (Feminist Africa, issue 12)*, 2009.

28 C Sachs, Feminist food sovereignty: crafting a new vision, paper presented at the International Conference on Food Sovereignty: A Critical Dialogue, Yale University, New Haven, 14–15 September 2013.

29 A Hayes-Conroy & J Hayes-Conroy, Visceral difference, feelings and social boundaries in slow food, in A Hayes (ed.), *Bodily geographies of 'slow' food: food activism and visceral politics*, Clark University, Worcester, 2009; A Hayes-Conroy & J Hayes-Conroy, Taking back taste: feminism, food and visceral politics, *Gender, Place & Culture: A Journal of Feminist Geography*, 15, 2008, 1.

30 A Hayes-Conroy & J Hayes-Conroy, Visceral difference, feelings and social boundaries in slow food, in A Hayes (ed.), *Bodily geographies of 'slow' food: food activism and visceral politics*, Clark University, Worcester, 2009.

31 R Patel, *Stuffed and starved: the hidden battle for the world food system*, New York: Melville House, 2008.

32 S Arnold, Preface, in S Arnold & A Nitecki (eds.), *Culture and development in Africa*, Trenton: Africa World Press, 1990, vii.

33 A Desai, *Fasting, feasting*, London: Chatto and Windus, 1999.

34 G Vahed & T Waetjen, *Gender, modernity and Indian delights: the women's cultural group of Durban: 1954–2010*, Cape Town: HSRC Press, 2010.

35 S Harding, *Whose science? Whose knowledge? Thinking from women's lives*, New York: Cornell University Press, 1991, 121.

36 P Hill Collins, *Black feminist thought: knowledge consciousness, and the politics of empowerment*, 2nd ed., New York: Routledge, 2000, 251.

37 Swaans, Broerse, Meincke, Mudhara and Bunders (2009). Promoting food security and well-being among poor and HIV/AIDS affected households: lessons from an interactive and integrated approach. Eval Program Plann. 2009 Feb;32(1):31-42. doi: 10.1016/j.evalprogplan.2008.09.002. Epub 2008 Sep 24.

38 S Barry (director), *I'm not done yet!*, 2014.

39 M Malan, SA's the fattest sub-Saharan nation, *Mail and Guardian*, 29 May 2014.

40 LH Weasel, Conducting research from the ground up, *International Review of Qualitative Research*, 4, 2011, 417.

A case study of gender and security sector reform in Zimbabwe

Netsai Mushonga

This article explores gender and security sector reform (SSR) in Zimbabwe from 2008 to the present. It firstly postulates that the purpose of gender-sensitive SSR is to transform security services so as to enhance human security, as opposed to having an exclusive focus on state and territorial security. A comprehensive analysis of the policy and legislative framework governing gender and SSR at the global, continental, sub-regional and national levels will be presented, followed by the argument that efforts to reform the partisan and oftentimes non-professional tendencies of the security sector – especially the Zimbabwe Defence Forces, Zimbabwe Republic Police, Central Intelligence Organisation and Zimbabwe Prison Services – to promote democracy have met with firm resistance. However, gender-sensitive SSR has made significant headway in Zimbabwe since it is considered less threatening by the government. It should be noted, nevertheless, that gender-sensitive SSR has the potential to shift levels of professionalism and accountability within the sector as well as change attitudes to enhance security at the personal and communal levels. The process can gradually increase the percentage of women serving in the security sector. In conclusion, recommendations are made to broaden and deepen gender-sensitive SSR as the only viable alternative in the current political environment in Zimbabwe.

Introduction

Zimbabwe has comprehensive legislative and policy frameworks to enhance women's security, but women have difficulty accessing the requisite security. The biggest threat to the security of women and girls in Zimbabwe is gender-based violence (GBV), which, according to the baseline survey by Gender Links and the Ministry of Women Affairs, Gender and Development, is an extensive problem.[1] In the baseline study, 68% of all women interviewed had experienced some form of violence at least once in their lifetime and 46% of men revealed that they had perpetrated violence at least once in their lifetime.[2] Zimbabwean women have reported that in some instances security forces are the perpetrators of this violence and that this diminishes their credibility as protectors.[3] Women face additional constraints, such as lacking the financial resources to travel to police stations, pay lawyers and access the courts, where the justice delivery system is generally slow. Women have also been victims of the politically-motivated violence that flares up in each electoral cycle. Levels of politically-motivated violence spiralled in 2008, when it is estimated that 36 000 people were internally displaced, 5 000 people were beaten and tortured, and 200 people were killed.[4] These issues were not addressed during the period of the Government of National Unity (GNU), and no visible efforts have been made to hold perpetrators accountable.

Efforts to reform the partisan and oftentimes unprofessional tendencies of the security sector – especially the Zimbabwe Defence Forces (ZDF), Zimbabwe Republic Police (ZRP), Central Intelligence Organisation (CIO) and Zimbabwe Prison Services (ZPS) – have met with resistance. However, gender-sensitive security sector reform (SSR) has made significant headway in Zimbabwe as it is considered less threatening by the government. Gender-sensitive SSR, however, has the potential to shift levels of professionalism and accountability within the sector, as well as changing attitudes to enhance security at the personal and communal levels. The process can gradually increase the percentage of women serving in the security sector. In conclusion, recommendations will be made on how to broaden and deepen gender-sensitive SSR in the current political environment in Zimbabwe.

Brief overview of legal and policy frameworks

The African Union (AU) Policy Framework on Security Sector Reform (2012) and the Southern Africa Development Community (SADC) Protocol on Gender and Development (2008) are key frameworks influencing gender and SSR processes in Zimbabwe. One of the core principles of the AU's policy is gender equality and women's empowerment,[5] while the SADC Protocol calls for the implementation of United Nations Security Council Resolution (UNSCR) 1325.[6]

Zimbabwe has a new policy framework that was ushered in by the promulgation of a new national constitution in May 2013. The Constitution espouses gender balance in governance and leadership positions, and mandates the state to 'take positive measures to rectify gender discrimination and imbalances resulting from past practices and policies', thus prescribing affirmative action measures.[7] The supreme law also legislates the rights to security, human dignity and freedom from torture or cruel, inhuman and degrading treatment or punishment. The state should promote gender balance in national security institutions and ensure the human security of women as constitutional mandates. The constitution demands that the security services become non-partisan, desist from supporting political interests, and not be active members or office bearers of any political party or organisation.[8] This is a progressive development, since the leadership of the ZDF, ZRP and ZPS have in the past publicly declared allegiance and support to the ruling political party, the Zimbabwe African National Union – Patriotic Front (ZANU-PF).[9]

However, although the national constitution reflects gender balance, gender is not mainstreamed in legislation and policies governing the ZDF, ZRP and ZPS.

Women and the security sector in Zimbabwe

The security sector inherited many challenges in promoting the security of women, girls and their communities. Before independence, the sector played a critical role in implementing the repressive policies of the colonial state.[10] During this time, ZRP personnel had 'extensive powers to arrest, detain and operated as an extension of the army, enforcing curfews and engaging in combat'.[11] The different components that now comprise the ZDF have a history of brutalising civilians with impunity during the liberation war, and this trend continued into the era of independence.[12]

After the ruling ZANU-PF party began to lose popular support, the security sector was increasingly used for partisan political purposes.[13] Security sector personnel, especially the ZDF, ZRP and CIO, have been accused of being 'highly partisan and engaging in gross human rights abuses, violence, torture and intimidation of political opponents and civic activists'.[14]

Several surveys and consultations have revealed that the majority of women and girls do not trust and are afraid of personnel in the security sector.[15] There have been widespread reports of GBV perpetrated by security sector personnel, calling into question their role as 'protectors'. In a baseline survey conducted in 2012 to assess the perceptions of ordinary women and girls on the efficacy of state security services in enhancing their security, 65% of respondents indicated that they were not satisfied with the police services (see Figure 1).[16] The 2013 Violence Against Women Baseline Survey highlighted that only one in fourteen women who are physically abused reported the abuse to the police, and only one in seven female rape victims reported their cases.[17] A study conducted by the Southern Africa Litigation Centre found that the police tend to target and harass women suspected of being commercial sex workers, whom they tend to abuse.[18]

Women complain that the ZRP lacks follow through, selectively prosecutes cases and makes procedural shortcuts in investigations.[19] The ZRP has therefore failed to fully implement existing legislation, like the Domestic Violence Act. GBV is a major threat to the security of women and girls in the country and the ZRP has a responsibility to prevent and mitigate it.

The ZPS runs prisons that are overcrowded and are a cause of great concern to human rights activists. In 2009, it was reported that an average of six prisoners were dying per day at Chikurubi Prison due to a combination of unhygienic conditions and a lack of adequate nutrition and health care services.[20] Women in police custody report that the prison conditions are not gender sensitive as there is a lack of suitable bathrooms, sanitary ware and disposal facilities.[21] The ZPS operates with inadequate space for the growing number of prisoners and lacks basics such as adequate food and health facilities.

Characteristics of the security sector in Zimbabwe

As can be seen in Table 1, it is estimated that women constitute approximately 20% of ZDF personnel.[22] The majority of women are, however, concentrated in the lower ranks of the ZDF. The first female Brigadier General, Shailet Moyo, was promoted to the rank in 2013.

Figure 1   **Level of women's satisfaction with police services**

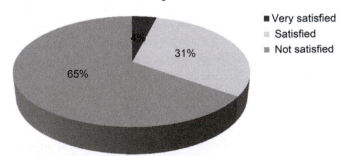

Source   Women's Coalition of Zimbabwe, *Baseline study: perceptions of ordinary women and girls on the efficacy of state security service sector in enhancing their security*, April 2012.

Table 1 Main features of the security sector in Zimbabwe

	Zimbabwe Defence Forces	Zimbabwe Republic Police	Zimbabwe Prison Services	Central Intelligence Organisation
Total staff	35 000[23]	25 000[24]	5 000[25]	8 000–10 000[26]
Percentage of female representation among staff	20%	25%	Data not available; however, women constitute 50% of assistant commissioners and overall representation is less than 30%.	Unknown.
Legislation	Zimbabwe Defence Forces Act of 1997, which is not gender mainstreamed nor aligned to the new constitution.	Police Force Act of 1975, which is not gender mainstreamed nor aligned to the new constitution.	Zimbabwe Prisons Act 4 of 1993, which is not gender mainstreamed nor aligned to the new constitution.	No direct legislation; there is a need to craft new policies and legislation guided by the new constitution.
Gender sensitive policies and features	None	Sexual Harassment Policy, Victim Friendly Units, the ZRP Women's Police Network.	Gender focal person.[27]	Unknown.
Constitutional Mandate	To protect Zimbabwe, its people, its national security and interests and its territorial integrity, and to uphold the Constitution.[28]	To protect and secure the lives and property of the people, and to detect, investigate and prevent crime.[29]	To protect society from criminals through the incarceration and rehabilitation of convicted persons, and others who are lawfully required to be detained, and their reintegration into society.[30]	Unclear

The police, at 25%, have a slightly better representation of women.[31] They have also adopted a sexual harassment policy and have a victim friendly unit to deal with the survivors of GBV. Police-women also launched their own network in 2009 with the goals of 'providing a platform to work towards enhancing cooperation, coordination, sharing best practices, expertise, skills, challenges and solutions on gender issues in the police force'.[32] There has therefore been some attempt at gender mainstreaming within the ZRP.

Although the percentage of women in the ZPS is unknown, a gender balance has been achieved at the level of assistant commissioner. The ZPS also has a gender-focal person who is tasked with promoting gender equality.[33] Lastly, with the CIO, not much is known about gender mainstreaming.

Zimbabwe has done well in terms of the participation of women in peacekeeping. Personnel from the ZDF and ZRP have participated in international peacekeeping missions and the country has done well in the representation of women in their contingents. In the 2014–15 season, women comprised 35% of Zimbabwe's contingent sent for UN peacekeeping missions, the highest ratio of women to men in the SADC region for that year.[34] The country has attained a record of excellence in its peacekeeping work on the African continent,[35] and this is indicative of the fact that the security sector has the potential to deliver the same quality of service internally.

Gender-sensitive SSR

After the 2000 constitutional referendum, land reform and elections, the 'gender machinery' and women's movement in Zimbabwe realised the need for gender-sensitive SSR that would trans-form the internal structures of security sector institutions, afford women greater participation and ensure effective oversight. Similarly, there was a need to empower women to demand protec-tion and redress their security concerns about the police, as well as actively engaging in the SSR discourse. The new constitution now calls for effective executive, parliamentary and judicial over-sight of the security sector, and this should be made a reality.

Civil society engagements with security sector personnel, though sporadic at first, have become more systematic as trust and confidence levels have increased between the stakeholders. The women's movement and civil society organisations have held consultations with senior personnel from the security sector on the support they need for effective gender mainstreaming.

Other internal gender mainstreaming activities have included raising awareness about human rights and gender training for all arms of the security sector. Activity to raise awareness about the Domestic Violence Act and the responsibilities of police officers has increased since the promul-gation of the act in 2007. Civil society has carried out gender audits of the curricula of national security courses and made suggestions for making them more gender sensitive. There has also been advocacy for involving increasing numbers of women in peacekeeping missions. Another critical initiative consists in the action research undertaken by the African Community Publishing and Development Trust that facilitated a constructive dialogue between women, men, traditional leaders and security sector actors, especially the police and army.[36] The action research produced a resource manual to guide this work and replicate it around Zimbabwe. The women's movement carried out a baseline survey of the perception of women around the efficacy of the services of the various security sector institutions and this report was shared with the leadership of the sector. The gender machinery and women's movement has involved women from the security sector in women's rights advocacy functions such as commemorations of International Women's Day and the 16 Days of Activism against GBV. Women from the security sector were also engaged and consulted in raising awareness and strategy meetings during the constitution-making process of 2009–13. Since the promulgation of the new constitution, the women's movement has begun to push for a realignment of legislation and policies governing the security sector.

Does integrating women enhance their security?

Mainstreaming gender during SSR is a long process of building trust and transforming the security sector into an institution that serves as a source of security for women and girls – and ultimately the whole community. It is critical to attain higher levels of representation of women in the sector, but these numbers should never be conflated with gender sensitivity. Currently the security sector has less than 30% women in their structures and all evidence points to the fact that the cultures of the institutions have remained predominantly patriarchal. Gender mainstreaming requires that the work goes deeper than the numbers, to transform the political orientation of the sector, the sexist and violent institutional cultures,[37] and the patriarchal attitudes of the security sector, and get them to appreciate the human rights of women and girls. The gender approach should guide work to challenge the link between masculinity, violence and domination to promote cultures of peace, unity and cooperation. The security sector in Zimbabwe has largely remained partisan and patriarchal and, in some instances, poses a serious threat to women's security rather than safeguarding it.[38]

Gender mainstreaming in the security sector has predominantly been focused on women. This is problematic as it creates a situation where the responsibility of creating a more secure environment is shifted solely onto female officers. This is not a viable strategy, as it is necessary to work with all personnel to ensure transformation. Some of the champions of the work to prevent, protect and mitigate against GBV are male officers who have received awareness training on the subject.[39] However, the strategies to support women's networks in the security sector are viable and constructive. Such efforts should include facilitating national and international network building and sharing best practices.

Recommendations

- Conduct a gender audit of security sector legislation and policies with a view to amending them so that they are in line with the new constitution, as well as SADC and AU policies on women, peace and security. The policies should include affirmative action measures to recruit more women and accelerate their rise to higher ranks in the sector.[40]
- Make all training gender sensitive by auditing the security sector curricula and training materials and amending them accordingly. In-service training in gender and human rights should be offered to all staff.
- Advocate for the allocation of extra human and financial resources for implementing security legislation such as the Domestic Violence Act and other policies and legislation that enhance women's security.
- Support informal security sector institutions such as municipal police, religious leaders, chiefs and headmen to become more gender sensitive.[41]
- Introduce gender focal points to give technical advice as well as monitor progress of gender mainstreaming in all security sector institutions.

- Advocate for 50/50 gender balance of women in the National Peace and Reconciliation Commission to push a gender-sensitive peace and security agenda.
- Advocate for the recruitment, retention and promotion of women in national-level security sector institutions.
- Support regional and national networks of women in the security sector to allow active internal advocacy for gender equality in all facets of the sector.
- Professionalise the security sector to become non-partisan so that it serves ordinary citizens with diligence.

Notes

1 M Machisa and S Chingamuka (eds.), *Peace begins at home: violence against women (VAW) baseline study Zimbabwe*, Johannesburg: Ministry of Women Affairs, Gender and Community Development and Gender Links, 2013.

2 Ibid.

3 T Murithi and A Mawadza (eds.), *Zimbabwe in transition: a view from within*, Cape Town: Institute of Justice and Reconciliation, 2011.

4 Embassy of the United States, Human rights report 2011: Zimbabwe, http://harare.usembassy.gov/human_rights_report_2011.html (accessed 10 August 2015).

5 African Union, Policy framework on security sector reform, www.peaceau.org/uploads/au-policy-framework-on-security-sector-reform-ae-ssr.pdf (accessed 15 July 2015).

6 Southern African Development Community, Protocol on gender and development, www.sadc.int/files/8713/5292/8364/Protocol_on_Gender_and_Development_2008.pdf (accessed August 2015).

7 Constitution of Zimbabwe Amendment (No. 20) Act of 2013, chapter 2, section 17.

8 Ibid., chapter 4, sections 51–53.

9 E Muller, Obstacles to reforming Zimbabwe's security sector, www.ssrresourcecentre.org/2014/04/24/obstacles-to-reforming-zimbabwes-security-sector/ (accessed August 2015).

10 Women's Coalition of Zimbabwe, *Baseline survey: empowering women towards advocacy for implementation of Article 28 of the SADC Protocol on Gender and Development: gender equality and empowerment needs of women in state security service sector*, Harare: Women's Coalition of Zimbabwe, 2012, 11.

11 P Matsheza and G Mudzongo, *Implementing a human rights programme: SAHRIT's experiences with the Zimbabwe Republic Police*, Harare: SAHRIT, 2003.[AQ01]

12 C Hendricks and L Hutton, *Providing security and justice for the people of Zimbabwe: security sector reform in Zimbabwe*, Pretoria: Institute for Security Studies, 2009.

13 T Murithi and A Mawadza (eds.), *Zimbabwe in transition: a view from within*, Cape Town: Institute of Justice and Reconciliation, 2011.

14 M Nyakudya, Security sector reform in Zimbabwe: prospects cnd Challenges, www.solidaritypeacetrust.org/733/security-sector-reform-in-Zimbabwe-prospects-and-challenges/ (accessed 8 July 2015).

15 Women's Coalition of Zimbabwe, *Baseline study: perceptions of ordinary women and girls on the efficacy of state security service sector in enhancing their security*, Harare: Women's Coalition of Zimbabwe, 2012; Africa Community Publishing Trust, *Connecting and protecting: building constructive communication and relationships between women, men and the security services*, Harare: Fingertip Co-operative Limited, 2014.

16 Women's Coalition of Zimbabwe, *Baseline study: perceptions of ordinary women and girls on the efficacy of state security service sector in enhancing their security*, Harare: Women's Coalition of Zimbabwe, 2012.

17 M Machisa and S Chingamuka (eds.), *Peace begins at home: violence against women (VAW) baseline study Zimbabwe*, Johannesburg: Ministry of Women Affairs, Gender and Community Development and Gender Links, 2013.

18 Southern Africa Litigation Centre, Policing sex work in Zimbabwe – an appropriate response?, www.southernafricalitigationcentre.org/tag/sex-work/ (accessed 8 July 2015).

19 K Chitiyo, A case for security sector reform in Zimbabwe, 2009, www.rusi.org/downloads/assets/Zimbabwe-SSR-Report.pdf (accessed 8 July 2015).

20 Peta Thornycroft, Half of prisoners die of starvation in Zimbabwe jails, *The Telegraph*, 19 May 2009, www.telegraph.co. uk/news/worldnews/africaandindianocean/zimbabwe/5345106/Half-of-prisoners-die-of-starvation-in-Zimbabwe-jails.html

21 M Chiba, *An assessment of the compliance of conditions for female suspects held in custody in police stations in Harare with the 2013 Zimbabwe constitution*, Zimbabwe: Southern and Eastern Africa Regional Centre for Women's Law, 2014.

22 See the annual reports at the SADC gender protocol barometer, www.genderlinks.org.za/page/sadc-research (accessed 8 July 2015).

23 K Chitiyo, A case for security sector reform in Zimbabwe, 2009, www.rusi.org/downloads/assets/Zimbabwe-SSR-Report.pdf (accessed 8 July 2015).

24 Ibid.

25 Ibid.

26 Ibid.

27 Ibid.

28 Constitution of Zimbabwe Amendment (No 20) Act of 2013.

29 Ibid.

30 Ibid.

31 Ibid.

32 ZRP launches women's empowerment network, *AllAfrica*, 4 April 2009, www.allafrica.com/stories/200904060452. html

33 Women's Coalition of Zimbabwe, *Report of the women's roundtable consultation with leaders of the Security sector*, Harare: Women's Coalition of Zimbabwe, 2011.

34 SADC gender protocol barometer, www.genderlinks.org.za/page/sadc-research (accessed 8 July 2015).

35 K Chitiyo, A case for security sector reform in Zimbabwe, 2009, www.rusi.org/downloads/assets/Zimbabwe-SSR-Report.pdf (accessed 8 July 2015).

36 Africa Community Publishing Trust, *Connecting and protecting: building constructive communication and relationships between women, men and the security services*, Harare: Fingertip Co-operative Limited, 2014.

37 C Hendricks, Research on gender and SSR in Africa, in M Eriksson and M Utas (eds.), *Beyond 'gender and stir': reflections on gender and SSR in the aftermath of African conflicts*, Uppsala: The Nordic African Institute, 2012.

38 M Chiba, *An assessment of the compliance of conditions for female suspects held in custody in police stations in Harare with the 2013 Zimbabwe constitution*, Zimbabwe: Southern and Eastern Africa Regional Centre for Women's Law, 2014.

39 Africa Community Publishing Trust, *Connecting and protecting: building constructive communication and relationships between women, men and the security services*, Harare: Fingertip Co-operative Limited, 2014.

40 P Made, Southern Africa Development Community gender protocol barometer Zimbabwe, 2015, www.genderlinks. org/article/sadc-gender-protocol-barometer-2015-zimbabwe-2015.05.05 (accessed 15 July 2015).

41 Women's Coalition of Zimbabwe, *Baseline study: perceptions of ordinary women and girls on the efficacy of state security service sector in enhancing their security*, Harare: Women's Coalition of Zimbabwe, 2012.

Women police in the Nigerian security sector

Tosin Akinjobi-Babatunde

This article details the history and philosophy behind major changes in police tradition and organisation in Nigeria in 1955. Women in the Nigeria Police Force (NPF), influenced by their background as enforcers of societal norms, developed a type of social-work-oriented policing. Using primary and secondary sources of historical information, this article discusses the origin of women in the NPF, the specialised role of women in police work, and the changes that have been effected in the roles and functions of women in policing in Nigeria. Situated within the conceptual frameworks of patriarchy and gender, this article argues that gender biases impeded the incorporation of women into the police and, when eventually introduced, gender limitations constrained their roles, operations and activities.

Introduction

This article is situated within the conceptual frameworks of patriarchy and gender, both of which are useful in explaining the subordination of women in terms of power, status, employment and access to other resources in Nigeria. Gender explains the socially constructed difference between a man and a woman on the basis of their reproductive properties, while patriarchy emphasises the social exclusion of women, based on how the sexual composition of the body defines the social meaning and significance accorded women in the society.

In traditional Nigerian societies, police work was carried out by adult males who were engaged in the prevention and control of crime and disorder. Women played the primary role of socialisation, instilling discipline, morals and virtues in their children as part of the broader system of crime prevention and control in society. The display of deviant behaviour by children was often attributed to a lack of maternal care and supervision, a manifestation of the belief that women were 'naturally' capable of preventing and controlling crimes in the society. The policing philosophy and tradition of the colonial state also assigned policing as predominantly a task for adult males.[1] Proposed by the Nigerian Women's Party (NWP), changes were effected in policing tradition and organisation to establish the 'Women's Police Branch' (WPB) in 1955.

Between the early 1940s and 1955, women police in Nigeria went through the phases of integration, acceptance and development, facing a number of the same problems as women police throughout the world have faced, such as discriminatory provisions and limited opportunities for professional advancement.[2] However, in other ways, the Nigerian experience at that time was quite different to the rest of the world in that the reform of policing tradition and organisation resulted in the design of an unusual style of social-work-oriented policing, geared specifically towards policing women and children. This new style of policing was radically different from traditional policing operations. In effect, they moved beyond the emulation of the traditional male style of policing to the development of a new style of policing directed at securing the most vulnerable groups in society.

The following section describes the situation that warranted the entrance of women into police work and the organisational changes that took place in the Nigerian Police Force (NPF) as a result. The second section describes the specialised roles and the changes that have been effected in the roles of women in policing in Nigeria, as well as the challenges encountered while working to break the glass ceiling of this male-dominated profession. The third section illustrates the ongoing challenges facing women police in the NPF, and the conclusion discusses the implications of these changes and challenges for women in policing, as well as making some recommendations going forward.

Integration of women in policing in Nigeria

Although the role of women in traditional crime prevention and control has been overshadowed by the accounts of men and the events that shaped history,[3] women have been involved in the social systems of home, work and community control. The role of women as reproducers of societal norms and values has meant that there is often societal reference to what 'we learnt at our mothers' knees'. This means that society places a high level of importance, as well as expectation, on the behaviour of women – who are supposed to fulfil the responsibilities of caring and disciplining – at home and in public. However, women's involvement in social control has not remained static. In order to meet the needs of women and children in trouble, women have supported formal agents of social control by enlisting in the police and other security sector institutions (SSIs).

The struggle for women's empowerment and equality that followed the end of colonial rule also gradually paved the way for women's integration into the police service. For 25 years after the establishment of the NPF in 1930, consequent to the amalgamation of the north and south protectorates' police forces,[4] no women police existed in Nigeria. Notably, women were not deemed fit for the rigours of police work until the increase in criminal activities involving women suggested a profound need for women police in crime prevention and control. As a result, the campaign for the enlistment of women in the police started.

The campaign began in November 1944, when a delegation of the political and social sections of the NWP advocated for the recruitment of female constables during talks with the chief secretary to the colonial government, A E T Benson,[5] and the police commissioner at the time, C W King. The delegation proposed that women aged 40 to 50 years be employed as police constables 'because they would be better able than men to prevent prostitution and deal with female criminals'.[6] Through such acceptance it was hoped that the police would take on greater social services missions. The proposal was objected to on the grounds that women of such an age would not be able to perform the tasks suggested, and there were strong Islamic sentiments against this proposition among the elite in the north.[7] Although the proposal was not accepted, the NWP did not relent in advocating for effecting changes to the NPF's traditions and organisation in order to integrate women.

In the early 1950s, about the same time that the NWP was reopening discussions on the issue of women in the police force, events outside Nigeria were pointing to a new consciousness that could not be ignored by the colonial administration. On 2 December 1949, the United Nations (UN) Economic and Social Council (ECOSOC) had secured an international protocol for the suppression of trafficking in persons, especially young girls and women, into prostitution. The convention so adopted required the governments of the world to show adequate sensitivity to the need for women police to assist in the prevention of prostitution and the protection of its victims. Between January and February 1953, the colonial government and the police authorities had before them a questionnaire from ECOSOC on the measures used to suppress trafficking in women and girls.[8] As there was no existing structure featuring women police, the colonial administration lacked the type of policewomen desired by ECOSOC. This development compounded the pressure on the colonial administration, as well as the police authorities, regarding the need to enlist women in the police.

The proposal of the NWP and the international consciousness of the need for women to take the lead in suppressing the trafficking of women and children prompted various interest groups and political representatives to support the need for changes in police traditions and organisation. Subsequently, the colonial government announced its decision to establish the 'Women's Police Branch'.

The advert for the recruitment of women police appeared in newspapers in August 1955.[9] Qualification for enlistment emphasised physical ability, a minimum educational standard, and a security check that assessed character and past records through references and a fingerprint check.[10] In the end, the general minimum height qualification of five feet, six inches was waived for women who were two inches shorter, while the test of overall medical fitness was upheld.[11] The minimum educational attainment of standard six (now primary six) or the modern–two certificate was waived for recruits from the north.[12] The screening process relied heavily on physical ability rather than verbal communication skills or a background in problem-solving, as is needed in community-oriented policing where citizens are identified as 'clients' to be served and policing involves more communication skills and negotiating ability. The recruitment criteria failed to correlate morality and the psychological, communication and negotiation skills used in traditional social control with law enforcement. It is pertinent to note that the police service and most other SSIs in the country are yet to change their hiring processes to reflect the reality of modern methods of crime prevention. Given the changes in technology and procedure, it is necessary to find ways other than physical ability to assess applicants' suitability for policing.

Female recruits were expected to be unmarried until they received permission to marry after serving for a period of three years.[13] This remains unchanged under the Nigerian Police Act of 1967, which decrees that – while male police officers are not subjected to any marital restrictions – a woman police officer is not free to decide when to marry and may be subjected to a long period of courtship, depending on her length of service. The suitor must pass a test of good character, after being subjected to 'surveillance', which depends on the subjective evaluation of the Commissioner of Police. Pioneer women police were trained in Western dressing and footwear, gymnastics, swimming, lifesaving, first aid, fire and ambulance drills, police duties, court procedure, law of evidence, criminal law, penal code and field training, with the exception of arms drills. Firearms were considered unnecessary for the roles undertaken by women police, who were considered too weak to handle firearms. In the late 1980s, women police successfully agitated against their exclusion from arms drills.[14] With the expansion of the scope of modern police work and improvement in the tools of crime, women police now train with, have access to, and carry and use firearms, as well as being tutored on violent confrontation in anti-crime duties. Although changes have been effected in women's involvement in arms drills as part of their response to the exigencies of modern police work, this has not been institutionalised in police legislation and regulations.

The selection and interviewing of the 20 women who were considered fit enough for the positions and rigors of law enforcement was personally made by the inspector-general of police at the time, R J P McLaughlan. The first task of the pioneer policewomen was to take care of female prisoners and juveniles and to obtain their statements. These policewomen were employed for investigation duties with the railway police and at the police headquarters in matters involving women and children.[15] The distinction between social-work-oriented roles for policewomen as opposed to the traditional masculine roles of police officers established a gendered segregation in police work, but nevertheless initiated specialised responsibilities and compounded the social duties of women in the police.

In recent years, there has been an increase in the number of women in the police force, from 6 900 (5%) in 1993 to 36 128 (12,4%) in 2010, but they are concentrated in the lower ranks.[16] In July 2010, UNIFEM data indicated that 97,41% of the female police staff occupied low ranks, compared to 93,02% of their male colleagues; 936 of the 18 745 senior officers were women (5%).[17] The effort to recruit women into police work may have been energised by the drive for equal opportunities for women, the lack of employment opportunities, and the desire for a government bureaucracy that represents all segments of the population. Women have also benefited from demographic changes; the total number of people employed has increased dramatically and so women have filled the gaps, particularly as the supply of male workers has not been adequate enough to meet the rising demand.

The changing role of policewomen in Nigeria

A total of 20 women started the WPB, and their number increased slowly but steadily over time, standing at 170 between 1955 and 1962.[18] The pioneer policewomen used their duties in the police force to establish a juvenile welfare centre, in an atmosphere different from the ordinary police stations.[19] Over the years, policewomen have headed the juvenile welfare centres in all the divisional police headquarters. These centres serve as part-time counselling centres, where women function more as arbitrators and counsellors than hardnosed law enforcement agents.

The public, as well as male police officers in the force, initially resented 'the intrusion of women constables into what had been purely a male establishment'.[20] The pioneer policewomen were faced with profoundly discriminatory attitudes, as they were poorly represented and not given opportunities equal to those received by their male colleagues. They were also confronted with challenges in the areas of marriage, maternity and posting (as posting affects the upbringing of their children, their education and their overall well-being). Women could not initially rise beyond the rank of chief superintendent of police and many pioneers were retired from the service at that position until the embargo was lifted during the tenure of President Shehu Shagari. These challenges are still noticeable in the police force, and policewomen are networking to combat the problems they face in the profession. However, despite the challenges and hazards associated with the profession, a vast number of women police have distinguished themselves.[21]

Women in the NPF have made a departure from the conventional attachment to children- and women-related duties to other, diverse areas of policing. The scope of police work for women has widened and they have ventured into the 'frontlines' of law enforcement.[22] They are now engaged in surveillance, the prevention and detection of crimes, the prosecution of criminals, community policing, and peacekeeping.[23] Since the establishment of the human trafficking section of the NPF in 2000, it has been headed by women officers who 'have worked extremely hard to raise national profile and international reputation'.[24] Women have also held high positions in the administrative structure of the police – up to the level of the deputy inspector general of police – but no woman has been appointed the inspector general of police in Nigeria and very few have been commissioners of police. In 2007, less than 2% of the station, command, division and area commands were headed by women.

In 2004, the police established a female mobile unit to further protect women and children in the population. The unit has 46 squadrons; each squadron is comprised of about 2 000 mobile policewomen. Their duties are to constantly engage in arms and riot drills, internal security and mob dispersion, especially of riots and demonstrations involving women. It is their obligation to provide security for visiting first ladies, at international women's conferences – particularly when women dignitaries are in attendance – and at international events such as the All-Africa games. The most recent expansion of the roles of policewomen in the NPF is in their involvement in peacekeeping operations in Kosovo, East Timor, Liberia, Congo and the Sudan.

Ongoing challenges

Gender relations and the status of policewomen in Nigeria have either been grounded in laws and policies and/or patriarchal attitudes. The positions women occupy within the police force depend to a large extent on the individual goodwill of successive police chiefs and their disposition towards women.

The existing Police Act and Police Regulations (1990) view and treat women 'as not on an equal standing with men'.[25] Sections 121–125 and 127–128 are biased against women. As previously mentioned, there is discrimination in terms of the conditions of employment (e.g., the right to get married and have children) and there is an under representation of women in the service as a whole, but specifically in senior positions.

The police services are also seen as insensitive to the plight of victims of sexual and gender-based violence. They have been criticised for being unwilling to intervene in the protection of women and girls in 'domestic disputes', especially in 'more traditional areas of the country' and in cases where 'the level of alleged abuse does not exceed customary norms in the areas'.[26] Not only do the police ridicule and trivialise cases of domestic violence and rape reported to them, but they go further and actually blame the victims for their victimisation.[27] Police personnel have been identified as lacking the knowledge and skills to respond sensitively to gender-based crimes or to deal with vulnerable groups such as children and persons with disabilities, as they have received no training in policing such groups. The inclusion of women has therefore not had the desired impact of changing gender relations within the services and of increasing the security of women in society as a whole.

Conclusion

This article examined the integration of women into the NPF, the conventional roles of women in police work and the changing roles of women in policing in Nigeria since 1955. Using the conceptual frameworks of patriarchy and gender, the article argues that gender biases hindered the integration of women into police work until 25 years after the establishment of the NPF. Sexual prejudice, discrimination and exclusion further constrained the roles of women police to the specialised duties of policing women and children. Women police have recently experienced a shift from their traditional limited functions to include other forms of police work, but such changes are not grounded in the police regulations. Although the NPF has had women in its employ for a very long time, there is still a lot that needs to be done to create a police service that is gender sensitive and gender responsive. This includes introducing specialised programmes and units to deal with sexual and gender-based violence, revising laws, police regulations and the police training curriculum, and ensuring more gender-sensitive recruitment exercises. Moreover, given the changing nature of crime and conflict – for example, cybercrime, terrorism and violent extremism – much of which is targeted at women, the retraining of all police, but especially women police, in order to meet these new challenges is critical.

Acknowledgement

I would like to thank my supervisor, Dr. Kemi Rotimi, who provided insight and expertise that greatly assisted this research. I am also immensely grateful to Professor Cheryl Hendricks for comments that improved this manuscript.

Notes

1 M Weber, *Economy and society*, Oakland, CA: University of California Press, 1968.

2 Before 1975, women police were consigned to a separate division but in practice were dispersed throughout the British system. Women recruited in the India police service were generally assigned to reception work; see PG Shane, *Police and people: a comparison of five countries*, St. Louis, MO: C. V. Mosby, 1980.

3 G Vickers, Women's place: images of womanhood in the SBC, 1888–1929, master's dissertation, Vanderbilt University, Nashville, TN, USA, 1986.

4 K Rotimi, *The police in a federal state: the Nigerian experience*, Ibadan: College Press, 2001.

5 The members of the delegation were: Mrs T. Dedeke, Mrs A. Manuwa (Hon. Secretary), Mrs Ekemode (Treasurer), Mrs Coker, Mrs B. Oyediran, Mrs L. Timson and Mrs E. Kuti-Okoya; extracted from TN Tamuno, *The police in modern Nigeria, 1861–1965*, Ibadan: Ibadan University Press, 1970.

6 TN Tamuno, The police in modern Nigeria, 1861-1965, Ibadan: Ibadan University Press, 1970, 135.

7 Northern women were mostly in purdah and were basically housewives not meant to take up paid work or leave the home.

8 UNESCO took this action to secure the implementation of the international convention for the suppression of trafficking in persons and of the exploitation of the prostitution of others. The convention was adopted on 2 December 1949.

9 I Okoronko, Women police and the future of law enforcement in Nigeria, in A Solomon and I Iheanyi (eds.), *Policing Nigeria in the 21st century*, Ibadan: Spectrum Books, 2007.

10 TN Tamuno, *The police in modern Nigeria, 1861–1965*, Ibadan: Ibadan University Press, 1970.

11 Ibid.

12 Modern school was established as an intermediate three-level class between primary and secondary school. Modern two was the second level within the modern school's three levels. Western education was introduced much later in the north, as Islamic education was favoured over Western education.

13 Section 124 of the 1990 Police Acts states: 'A woman police officer who is desirous of marrying must first apply in writing to the commissioner of police for the State Police command in which she is serving, requesting permission to marry and giving the name, address, and occupation of the person she intends to marry. Permission will be granted for the marriage if the intended husband is of good character and the woman police officer has served in the force for a period of not less than three years.'

14 Interview with Mrs Bosede Dawodu, Deputy Commissioner of Police (DCP), Police Headquarters, Zone 11, Osogbo, 13 July 2011; interview with Mrs Florence Adebanjo, retired Deputy Inspector General of Police (DIG), 11 July 2011.

15 TN Tamuno, *The police in modern Nigeria, 1861–1965*, Ibadan: Ibadan University Press, 1970.

16 PB Dayil and A Sjoberg, Nigeria, in M Gaanderse and K Valasek (eds.), *The security sector and gender in West Africa: a survey of police, defence, justice and penal services in ECOWAS states*, Geneva: DCAF, 2011; A Holvikivi, Summary and analysis of findings, in in M Gaanderse and K Valasek (eds.), *The security sector and gender in West Africa: a survey of police, defence, justice and penal services in ECOWAS states*, Geneva: DCAF, 2011.

17 PB Dayil and A Sjoberg, Nigeria, in M Gaanderse and K Valasek (eds.), *The security sector and gender in West Africa: a survey of police, defence, justice and penal services in ECOWAS states*, Geneva: DCAF, 2011.

18 EP Alemika, Colonialism, state and policing in Nigeria, in *Crime, law and social change*, Nigeria: Centre for Law Enforcement Education in Nigeria (CLEEN) Foundation Papers, 1993.

19 RE Ezekiel-Hart, *Keepers of the peace (facts about the Nigeria police force)*, Lagos: Nigeria Police, 1962.

20 Ibid., op. cit., 26.

21 A number of women police have held the positions of the deputy inspector general of police and commissioner of police in various states in Nigeria. In 2007, a policewoman became the first Nigerian policewoman to become an Interpol commissioner.

22 I Okoronko, Women police and the future of law enforcement in Nigeria, in A Solomon and I Iheanyi (eds.), *Policing Nigeria in the 21st century*, Ibadan: Spectrum Books, 2007.

23 MAK Smith, The role of women in crime prevention, maintenance of law and peace and national security: an address at the inaugural National Executive Council meeting of the National Council of Women Societies, Abuja, 20 September 2001.

24 Ibid.

25 Federal Ministry of Women Affairs and Social Development, *National gender policy*, Abuja: Federal Ministry of Women Affairs and Social Development, 2007.

26 PB Dayil and A Sjoberg, Nigeria, in M Gaanderse and K Valasek (eds.), The security sector and gender in West Africa: a survey of police, defence, justice and penal services in ECOWAS states, Geneva: DCAF, 2011, 190.

27 Final Report of the Civil Society Panel on Police Reform in Nigeria, 2012, www.noprin.org/CSO%20Panel%20Final%20Report.pdf (accessed August 2015).

Madagascar

Paving the way to national 'fampihavanana' and lasting peace

Gaby Razafindrakoto

Despite a constitution that condemns discrimination, as well as positive efforts by all sta-keholders, Madagascar is still far from meeting the desired objectives of the Southern African Development Community (SADC) Protocol on Gender and Development, or any other relevant international instruments and conventions. The establishment of an Organising Technical Committee on security sector reform for Madagascar is a positive development, which will hopefully facilitate an understanding of the multiple facets of gender and security in Madagascar as well as advancing the implementation of the instruments calling for greater female participation in the security sector.

Introduction

Madagascar experienced much political instability and related violence during the first decade of this century. In March 2009, after a coup d'état, Andry Rajoelina was declared the president of the High Transitional Authority by the Supreme Court, paving the way for democratic presidential elections and the formation of the Fourth Republic. A new constitution was adopted by referendum in 2010, and in 2013 Hery Rajaonarimampianina was declared the winner in a presidential election that was deemed fair and transparent by the international community.

Despite these strides, the country still experiences latent and secular conflicts in addition to the legacy of various cyclical crises and the upheaval of the transitional period. While a return to constitutional order has been achieved, the population is far from enjoying human security.

The human security context

Although there is no open civil war in Madagascar, the majority of the country's citizens do not enjoy the full benefits of being at peace. There are frequent media reports of violence – such as the raids conducted by the Dahalo (cattle thieves) in the southern part of the country that have left villages deserted and halted productivity – as well as crimes that have become commonplace, including burglary, assault, kidnapping, and gender-based violence (GBV), all of which serve to undermine individual freedom and security. Insecurity also takes the form of the abject poverty faced by many in Madagascar, reinforced by chronic unemployment due to the closure of companies following the successive political crises. Unemployment levels have negatively impacted on households, in the form of marital or domestic violence, which again are reported almost daily in the local media.

Women within the human security context

Madagascar enshrined equality between men and women in its 2010 constitution. Madagascar became a party to the Convention on the Elimination of All Forms of Discrimination against Women (CEDAW) in 1989. It signed the Optional Protocol to the Convention in 2000, but has yet to ratify and accede to it. Similarly, Madagascar signed the Protocol to the African Charter on Human and Peoples' Rights on the Rights of Women in Africa in 2004. It has also signed the Southern African Development Community (SADC) Protocol on Gender and Development (2008), but this, too, has yet to be presented to parliament for ratification.

Madagascar has increased the representation of women in parliament. Women now have 21% of parliamentary seats, up from 13% in 2010.[1] This increase has been made possible with the support of international partners, including the United Nations Development Programme, which promoted the advancement of women and civil society organisations during the period of political crisis between 2009 and 2013.

The human insecurity described above has had a significant impact on the female population of Madagascar. Women are victims of both common crimes and raids (for example, by the Dahalos who take women as hostages). Statistics have shown that 21% of households in Madagascar are headed by women.[2] Although national statistics on GBV are not available, studies show that Madagascar has a high prevalence rate. For example, a study undertaken by the United Nations Population Fund (UNFPA) in three cities in Madagascar in 2011 indicated that 30% of the women had experienced GBV at least once in their lives.[3]

The departments responsible for victim support in cases of GBV do not have adequate resources to address the situation. In addition, there is no adequate structure available for sheltering GBV victims immediately following the attack; the heads of *Fokontanys* (villages or urban neighbourhoods), who are the primary recipients of GBV complaints at the community level, lack the capacity to deal with the issue; and, in many instances, families do not want GBV incidents to be made public and thus try to settle them privately. In such cases, victims' parents will often accept financial or in-kind compensation and the perpetrators are not legally sanctioned.

Women in the security sector in Madagascar

Article 28 of the SADC Protocol on Gender and Development provides for 'the equal representation of women in conflict resolution and peace processes, as well as the integration of a gender perspective in conflict resolution'.[4] The Protocol has specific goals to put in place measures to ensure that women have equal representation and participation in decision-making circles and positions, in conflict resolution and peacebuilding, in accordance with United Nations Security Council Resolution (UNSCR) 1325 on Women, Peace and Security.[5]

A recent report by the Joint Mission on Assessment Needs for Security Sector Reform (SSR) in the Republic of Madagascar, undertaken by the African Union (AU), provides insight into the extent of the gendered transformation of the security sector in Madagascar.[6] The Malagasy government requested this evaluation; a decision that reflects a deliberate choice to improve the sector so that it can meet the security needs of the population.

Within the criminal justice system, the report notes that, of the approximately 1 000 members of the body of magistrates, 50% are women. In corrections, 16% of prison officials are women, in the context of a prisoner population where 4,6% of the prisoners are women. In the National Police, only 11,6% of a total of about 8 000 police officers are women. Women recruited into the police, although in reduced numbers, are present at all levels of decision-making throughout the 93 police stations in 112 districts. The gender ratio for the gendarmerie is not available, although a quota system was implemented for two years. This quota system was to ensure the recruitment of 15% to 20% women for each budget item.[7] However, between 2009 and 2010, only 7% women were recruited, and the last promotion of 'women gendarmes' was in August 2014. At the level of national defence, there is no transformation in terms of gender equality. Comprised of approximately 22 000 men, the Malagasy military remains closed to women's integration into the existing system. The efforts made so far, which theoretically should have introduced a progressive 10% quota, reported a 0,1% actual percentage of women in the defence sector as a whole in 2013, and these women are located in the medical services.[8] Similarly, the Military Academy (which is the core of the army and gendarmerie training) does not have sufficient capacity to allow for the recruitment of a significant number of women or ensure their training.

Following this assessment, Decree No. 2015-144 setting up the Organising Technical Committee (OTC) on Security Sector Reform (SSR) was released on 23 February 2015. A woman has been appointed to establish the Permanent Secretariat of the OTC on SSR.[9] The members of the OTC will include various government and military representatives. The mission of the OTC is to organise a national seminar on SSR, preceded by regional ones.

Madagascar and UNSCR 1325

Numerous workshops and training sessions have been conducted in Madagascar around UNSCR 1325. The 'Gender, Peace and Security' cluster of the Southern Africa Gender Protocol Alliance, led by the Institute for Security Studies (ISS), organised a series of workshops on peace and security, held in 2010, 2011 and 2012. The third workshop developed a draft National Action Plan (NAP) on UNSCR 1325 for Madagascar. The Federation for the Promotion of Women and Children organised the 30/50 movement and the Network of Women Artisans of Peace have worked towards the implementation of UNSCR 1325 in Madagascar. The NAP is now in the process of being verified and adopted.

The NAP – the vision of which is to establish a developed country where peace, security and gender equality reign – focuses on six distinct pillars. It aims to facilitate the adoption and implementation of international, regional and national instruments, including UNSCR 1325. The creation of an enabling environment for gender equality and the protection of human rights are among the specific objectives of the NAP. To do this, existing laws need to be reviewed or amended with the intention of making them more gender sensitive.

The NAP calls for, among other imperatives, the following:

- Peace for all in every region, especially in the most remote areas, must be ensured through the deployment of more police units or gendarmerie to outlying posts.
- Specific measures to mitigate the impact of insecurity include: a concerted campaign to end the actions of Dahalo; reducing the proliferation of small arms; and the implementation of local conventions or 'dina' to maintain peace and security.
- Security sector personnel should be adequately trained and equipped.
- The development and implementation of an anti-corruption programme.
- The creation of structures for public feedback or collection to prevent security problems.
- The integration of civic education into the school curriculum to inculcate and maintain a culture of peace.
- Building, strengthening and empowering organisations and processes that can support peace, demand accountability, and ensure transparency at all levels.
- Increasing the participation of women in structures and processes for the prevention of conflict and management of conflict resolution mechanisms.
- Increasing the number of women in security sector institutions.
- Reducing GBV and HIV/AIDS, and eradicating poverty for sustainable development.[10]

More recently, women from 22 regions of Madagascar came together for a Dialogue of Malagasy Women on Reconciliation and Consolidation of Peace on 23–24 March 2015. There has, however, been a long process of mobilisation and intervention by women's groups in Madagascar to ensure gender equality and facilitate national reconciliation and greater human security. From the adoption of a 'Roadmap' (2010) by the disputing parties until the holding of the National Conference for National Reconciliation (2015), associations such as the Federation pour la Promotion Féminine et Enfantine, the Vondron'ny MIRALENTA ho an'ny Fampandrosoana, the National Council of Women of Madagascar and the Network of Women Artisans of Peace have worked tirelessly to demand access for and representation and participation of women in all consultative and decision-making bodies created to facilitate peace and security. However, despite the activism of civil society and rhetoric of state officials to mainstream gender into the security sector structures and processes, the results are still meagre.

Conclusion

The Constitution of the Fourth Republic of Madagascar calls for 'the elimination of all forms of injustice, corruption, inequality and discrimination' as a condition for the 'development of the personality and the identity of the Malagasy'.[11]

It is clear that despite the efforts of all stakeholders, Madagascar is still far from meeting the desired objectives of the SADC Protocol on Gender and Development, or any other relevant international instruments and conventions. Recent events in the Malagasy National Assembly, in which parliamentarians requested the impeachment of the president, illustrate that the road to political stability and social peace is difficult.

However, the right to security and lasting peace is part of the inalienable human rights of Malagasy women and girls. The establishment of the OTC on SSR for Madagascar and the results of the joint evaluation for the reform of the security sector in the country are positive developments. These will hopefully facilitate an understanding of the multiple facets of gender and security in Madagascar, as well as the implementation of the instruments calling for greater female participation in the security sector. Reforming the security sector requires the buy-in of the entire population, together with state security institutions; similarly, the role of civil society, traditional leaders and other non-state bodies should be reinforced. Effective and sustainable peace cannot be achieved without the vital role of civil society, to act as a 'watchdog' and monitor the implementation of any resolutions or laws related to peace and security matters. A federation or a platform should be set up and coordinated to ensure a systematic and concerted approach to this work. Finally, fostering a culture of peace and security through citizenship education, included in school curricula and through the appropriate training of security sector, may be the foundation of *fampihavanana*.

Notes

1 The World Bank, Proportion of seats held by women in national parliaments (%), http://data.worldbank.org/indicator/SG.GEN.PARL.ZS (accessed September 2015).

2 Encyclopedia of the Nations, Female headed households (% of households with a female head) – gender statistics, www.nationsencyclopedia.com/WorldStats/Gender-female-headed-households.html (accessed September 2015).

3 Small steps in Madagascar's fight against gender based violence, *IRIN*, 10 December 2013, www.irinnews.org/report/99304/small-steps-in-madagascar-s-fight-against-gender-based-violence (accessed September 2015).

4 SADC, SADC Protocol on Gender and Development, 2008, www.sadc.int/files/8713/5292/8364/Protocol_on_Gender_and_Development_2008.pdf (accessed September 2015).

5 Ibid.

6 *Cf Final_Rapport_de_la_Mission_d'Evaluation_Conjointe_à_Mada gascar_version_Francaise (1)(1) Avant propos §4* Unpublished. African Union, Final Report of the Joint Security Sector Assessment Mission for Madagascar, 2014, unpublished.

7 Ibid. See also Genderlinks, *SADC Gender Protocol Barometer*, Johannesburg: Genderlinks, 2014.

8 Ibid. See also Genderlinks, *SADC Gender Protocol Barometer*, Johannesburg: Genderlinks, 2014.

9 Le Conseil de Gouvernement du, Decret N 2015-144 Portant création du Comité Technique d'Organisation du séminaire national sur la réforme du secteur de la sécurité (RSS) du 23 février 2015.

10 Draft National Action Plan for the Implementation of UNSCR 1325 in Madagascar, 17 février 2015.

11 Parliament of Madagascar Constitution of the Fourth Republic of Madagascar, 2010, this draft action plan was developed by both civil society and government representatives at a workshop held on the 4-6 September 2012 in Antananarivo, Madagascar.

Sexual and gender-based violence in the Democratic Republic of Congo

Yolanda Sadie

Commitment by the government of the Democratic Republic of Congo to addressing sexual and gender-based violence (SGBV) in the country is reflected in a number of international commitments and national strategies. This article traces the (slow) progress in addressing some of the most important issues relating to SGBV to which the government has committed itself. It argues that unless the underlying gender norms and unequal power relations that form the basis of gender violence, discrimination and inequality in Congolese society are addressed, SGBV will persist.

Introduction

The history of the Democratic Republic of Congo (DRC) has been mired in violent conflict, particularly since Mobutu's fall from power in 1997. By the end of March 2009, an estimated 1,3 million people were displaced, mostly in provinces in the east – an area portrayed in the media as a place where 'hell is just a local call away'.[1] This was despite the peace agreements that took place in 2003 (Sun City Accords) and 2008 (Goma Accords).

Despite the February 2013 signing of yet another peace agreement – called the Peace, Security and Cooperation Framework for the Democratic Republic of Congo and the Region, also known as the Framework Agreement – by 11 African countries in Addis Ababa, under the auspices of the United Nations (UN) Secretary-General, and the fact that the notorious M23 rebel group was defeated in November 2013, little progress was made in 2014 to improve security for the population of the eastern DRC.

By the end of August 2013, the ongoing conflict in the east had further increased the number of displaced people to 2,7 million (compared to 2,2 million at the end of 2012).[2]

A well-known characteristic of this conflict, particularly in the eastern DRC, has been the use of sexual violence against women as a weapon of war, to the extent that it has been called the 'war within the war' and a war in which 'women's bodies are a battlefield [*le corps des femmes est un champ de bataille*]'.[3] The eastern DRC has also, for more than a decade, been described as the 'rape capital of the world', and was regarded by Margot Wallström (former UN Special Representative of the Secretary-General) as 'the worst place in the world to be a woman'.[4]

What needs to be underlined is that statistics on the extent of sexual and gender-based violence (SGBV) in the country are difficult to obtain due to the nature of the violence and logistical difficulties (poor infrastructure, poor communication and difficult terrain). Many cases also go unreported as a result of stigmatisation and victims' fear of reprisal. Since the late 1990s, numerous international and national organisations have published statistics on the number of incidences of sexual violence in the DRC, but little coordination (even within UN agencies) exists between them. Therefore, no form of systematic data collection (including by the government) currently exists in the country. However, despite the lack of accurate statistics, it is obvious from the available data that sexual violence (mostly against women and girls) exists on a large scale. For example, according to UN estimates, 200 000 women and girls were assaulted between 1997 and 2009, with more than 8 000 cases reported between January and September 2008 alone.[5] In the period January 2010 to December 2013, statistics collected by the United Nations Joint Human Rights Office (UNJHRO) from across its 18 field offices in the DRC show 3 635 incidences of sexual violence (rape and gang rape) by armed groups and/or state agents.[6] Of this, a total of 73% were women, 25% girls, and 2% men.[7] Of further significance is the fact that nearly half of the total number of incidences of sexual violence in this period were committed by the Congolese state agents, with the *Forces armées de la République du Congo* (FARDC) committing more than one third (35,24%) of the total number.[8] From January to September 2014, the United Nations Population Fund (UNFPA) recorded 11 769 cases of SGBV in the provinces of North Kivu, South Kivu, Orientale, Katanga and Maniema, of which 39% were considered to be directly related to the dynamics of armed conflict, perpetrated by armed individuals.[9]

A clear sign that neither the conflict nor the sexual violations against women by armed groups have abated in 2015 is, for example, the attack on Kikamba in South Kivu by an armed group on 1 May 2015 where over 100 women were raped. *Medicins sans Frontieres* claims that as many as 127 women sought medical attention after sexual assaults.[10]

Given the consistent high incidence of SGBV in the DRC, the fact that a substantial proportion of these attacks are committed by state agents, and the overwhelming emphasis placed on conflict-related sexual violence, this case study will address three important issues raised in recent scholarly contributions on SGBV in the country. In the first part, the implications of the strong focus on conflict-related sexual violence compared to the little attention paid to other acts of SGBV is highlighted. Against the background of government commitments to address SGBV, the second section addresses the lack of security sector reform, particularly with regard to the impunity of members of the armed forces who committed acts of sexual violence, the lack of accountability in the FARDC, and the under representation of women in the Congolese security and justice structures. In the last section, it is argued that addressing SGBV requires more than just institutional reform; it requires dealing with the cultural and customary origins and manifestations of the unequal power relations in Congolese society.

Challenging harmful stereotypes of SGBV

Though the acts of violence against women perpetrated by armed groups over the years can certainly not be ignored, very little attention is paid to other acts of SGBV; that is, those committed by, among others, partners, family members and community members. These include many other forms of SGBV apart from rape, such as sexual harassment, domestic violence, customary and cultural-related violence, and forced marriages.[11]

Statistics on these other forms of SGBV are difficult to obtain, but figures provided by the Ministry of Gender give some indication of the violence experienced by civilians in four provinces in the eastern DRC. These reveal that 35,4% of victims know their attackers, which include intimate partners, neighbours, community members, family members and classmates.[12] Freedman also highlights the fact that in areas that are now free of armed conflict, SGBV persists and, moreover, that there is an increasing proportion of incidences committed by civilians.[13] This single focus on rape perpetrated by armed groups, 'separate and outside other forms of violence' contributes to what Eriksson et al. argue as the 'ungendering' of other forms of violence that are committed on a large scale against civilians but receive much less attention.[14] In addition, Eriksson et al., as well as Freedman, highlight the resulting 'commercialisation of rape' that this single focus on rape by armed groups induces, which also becomes interwoven with survival strategies.[15] As Freedman argues, the strong focus on rape has created, on the one hand, a 'market' for services for rape victims that has led to organisations competing for the large amounts of international funding channelled into SGBV programmes;[16] and, on the other, to individuals recognising the 'benefits' of being perceived as a victim of rape (i.e., the survival strategies mentioned above).[17] Unfortunately, these incentives to 'victimhood' reinforce the gendered divide between women as the 'victims' and men as the 'perpetrators' of violence.[18]

Also important is the lack of recognition of male rape and other forms of sexual violence, and the fact that the current reporting of rape 'tends to strengthen existing gender power inequalities and stereotypes'.[19] Assessing the number of male rape victims is very difficult due to the extreme stigma attached, and statistics are likely to be higher than those reported by medical clinics.

Finally, and most importantly, the predominant focus on armed rape ignores the underlying sociocultural inequalities and discriminatory gender norms of violence. SGBV needs to be understood at its roots, and this entails taking into account the persistence of economic inequalities, discriminatory laws and customs, and the exclusion of women from political decision-making at all levels.[20]

Addressing sexual and gender-based violence

In view of the brief backdrop depicted above, it is important to focus on two broad aspects when assessing efforts and achievements over the years in addressing the issue of SGBV. These are: rape by armed forces, particularly the FARDC; and the existence of gender inequalities at all levels of society.

Commitments on paper by the government of the DRC to address SGBV are certainly not lacking. Besides being party to several international human rights instruments that require addressing crimes of sexual violence,[21] sexual violence has been criminalised under the Congolese Penal Code, which was amended in 2006. According to Zonge, the greatest achievement of the amendment is the provision of a 'modern, enlightened and gender-neutral definition of "rape"',[22] which is more stringent than that of the Rome Statute. In addition, the government adopted the National Strategy Against Gender Based Violence in 2009. In line with United Nations Security Council Resolutions (UNSCRs) 1325, 1820 and 1888, which the government has formally adopted, the National Strategy is structured around five elements:

- Combatting impunity;
- Protection and prevention;
- Security sector reform;

- Multi-sectoral assistance;
- Data gathering and mapping.[23]

In a press release in July 2014, President Kabila stated his commitment to 'further eradicating the systemic problem of sexual violence and the recruitment of children into armed groups' by appointing Jeanine Mabunda Lioko as his Special Representative on Sexual Violence and Child Recruitment.[24] In August 2014, the Congolese government launched a comprehensive action plan to tackle sexual violence by soldiers.

Two major problems that are repeatedly highlighted in reports, publications and scholarly contributions on SGBV in the DRC are the issues of impunity and the lack of accountability in the military, which are not only closely related but also underline the need for security sector reform.

Problems and achievements in combatting impunity

Over the years there have been allegations that the judicial system is beset with corruption, has limited capacity and is characterised by political interference. One of the problems is that magistrates often lack the proper training and basic equipment to conduct thorough investigations. Many of those arrested for rape also escaped from prison as a result of poor security and corruption among judicial and prison staff.[25] A very small proportion of victims of sexual violence make use of judicial assistance: for example, a study conducted by the Ministry of Gender found that only a third of victims (34,8%) made use of judicial assistance and the judiciary.[26] Lack of confidence in the judiciary, fear of intimidation, long distances to travel and a lack of financial means were provided as the main reasons for not accessing the official justice system. Medical, psychosocial and legal support is available only in and around provincial capitals.[27]

A concerning factor is that the justice sector only consists of 19,5% women. Women make up 6,3% of judges in the Supreme Court, 12% in the Appeal Courts and 20,4% in the District Courts and High Courts.[28] Of the 3 600 magistrates in the country, only 16% are women.[29]

In its Beijing+20 Evaluation Report, the Ministry of Gender notes some of the improvements to the judicial system: improvement in infrastructure and equipment, capacity in terms of dossiers and sensitising jurists and para-jurists to sexual violence, and establishing law clinics.[30]

In accordance with the Congolese Constitution (Article 156), the Military Judicial Code and the Military Criminal Code, the military justice system has exclusive jurisdiction over all acts of violence committed by the army, police and armed groups. Overall government statistics on the rate of prosecution by military courts are not available. However, the UNJHRO, which only started compiling data on prosecutions in July 2011, recorded 187 convictions (mostly of rape) by military courts in the period July 2011 to December 2013, of which 136 were members of the FARDC and 32 were members of the Congolese National Police (*Police Nationale Congolaise*, PNC). Only three of the FARDC members convicted were senior officials.[31] In 2014, military tribunals convicted 135 individuals of sexual violence: 76 members of the armed forces, 41 members of the national police, and 18 members of armed groups.[32]

As the UNJHRO notes, of particular concern is the impunity enjoyed by high-ranking officers alleged to be responsible for crimes of sexual violence – when cases do make it to trial, the outcome is often influenced by corrupt judicial figures or politicians.[33] However, a milestone in efforts at holding high-ranking officers to account is the convictions in 2014 of General Jerome Kakwavu and Lieutenant Colonel Engangela, with the former sentenced to 10 years for the war crimes of rape, murder and torture, and the latter given life imprisonment.[34]

In addition, very few members of armed groups responsible for sexual violence are ever arrested or prosecuted for a variety of reasons, including: the very difficult and remote terrain where they operate and where state authority does not exist; the difficulty of victims identifying perpetrators, particularly if they are from armed groups; and prosecutors fearing the escalation of tension and violence if members of armed forces are arrested and charged.[35]

However, on 31 March 2015, the FARDC signed a 'landmark' declaration that requires every commander serving in the FARDC to commit to a number of important actions, including: respecting human rights and international human law in relation to sexual violence in conflict; taking action against sexual violence committed by soldiers under their command; ensuring the prosecution of alleged perpetrators of sexual violence under their command; and facilitating access to areas under their command to military prosecutors and handing over perpetrators.[36] However, without a proper system of vetting current and future officers for having committed crimes of sexual violence and human rights abuses, little effect will be given to the above declaration. As Jean-Marie Guéhenno, president and chief executive officer of Crisis Group, remarks: 'Recruiting criminals to defeat other criminals, as it did in the past will not end the cycle of violence. Building a professional and accountable army will'.[37]

Congolese women in security sector reform

In its National Action Plan on UNSCR 1325 and 1820, the Congolese government commits itself to implementing the resolutions that promote women's equal participation in conflict prevention, peacebuilding, post-conflict reconstruction and decision-making at all levels. However, in practice this has not been realised. Women are highly under-represented in the Congolese security and justice structures and are virtually absent at the decision-making level.

The percentage of women included in peace-negotiating and peace-building teams over the past few years shows that women's voices are hardly a 'whisper'. At the 2013 negotiations in Addis Ababa, women constituted a mere 6,2%; as a result of the advocacy of women activists, this number increased to 12,5% during the national consultations held from 7 September to 5 October 2013 on strengthening national unity in the country.[38]

Women make up a very small proportion of the armed forces (2%), and in decision-making structures this drops to 1% women. Women in high-ranking positions in the police force are also under-represented, with 5,3% in positions ranging from assistant divisional inspectors to commissioners in 2012.[39]

Although the inclusion of women is regarded as an important component of security sector reform, simply recruiting women into the military and police forces will not curb the abuses by members of the security sector. As Eriksson Baaz argues, getting to the root of the problem requires a comprehensive approach, since the abuses perpetrated against civilians, and women in particular, should be considered in terms of 'deep-seated structural dysfunctions in the security forces'.[40] These include failed integration processes, unclear chains of command, hostile civil-military relations, and poor salaries.

Women as 'second-class citizens'

In the Gender Inequality Index of 2013, the DRC was ranked 147 out of 152 countries. This gives some indication of the gender inequalities that exist within all sectors of its society.

An important indicator in the progress of the implementation of the government's National Action Plan for UNSCR 1325 and women's status in society is the extent of their inclusion in decision-making positions in government. Women constitute a mere 10,8% of the National Assembly, 5,5% of the senate, 12% of ministers and 31,7% of secretary-generals in government departments.[41]

As mentioned above, SGBV cannot be addressed without addressing the cultural and customary origins and manifestations of the unequal power relations in Congolese society. The Family Code (which is in the process of being reviewed) establishes women as inferior – for example, Article 444 states that a wife must obey her husband and Article 448 stipulates that a woman has to obtain her husband's permission to effect any legal act for which she has to present herself in person.[42]

Although the Law on the Modalities of the Implementation of the Rights of Women, and Parity – which sets a quota of at least 30% of women in all public institutions and aims to ensure the implementation of the equal rights guaranteed by the Constitution – is in the process of being enacted, cultural norms and values in society will not change overnight.[43]

Conclusion

Addressing the DRC's high incidence of SGBV requires government engagement at multiple levels. Firstly, the government must show its commitment to dealing with all issues relating to SGBV in the country. Secondly, and more importantly, is the implementation of the commitments that have been undertaken over the last few years. These include the efforts at reforming state institutions (such as the judiciary and the security sector), providing support for victims of SGBV, and including women in all spheres of government decision-making. Though minor advances have been made, including the criminalisation of sexual violence under the Congolese Penal Code and some improvement in the prosecution of members of the security sector, SGBV shows no signs of decreasing.

Finally, addressing SGBV requires more than just institutional reform and 'adding' more women. It requires tackling the root causes of the problem, namely the existing gender norms and power relations in society. A start would be a change in the attitudes of both men and women with regard to 'women's and men's places' in society. In this regard 'adding more women' may indeed help. The more visible women become in public positions, the stronger the socialisation of attitudes on a woman's place and her capabilities.[44]

Notes

1 D Snow, The Democratic Republic of the Congo: where hell is just a call away, *The Independent*, 4 October 2013.

2 UNHCR, Democratic Republic of Congo, global appeal, 2015, www.unhcr.org/5461e5fd.pdf (accessed July 2015); Much aid, little long-term impact in DRC, *Irin News*, 27 January 2015, www.irinnews.org/report/101053/much-aid–long-term-impact-in-drc

3 Human Rights Watch, The war within the war, www.hrw.org/reports/2002/drc/Congo0602.pdf (accessed July 2015). Le corps des femmes est un champ de bataille, J D Kannah, *Le Parisien*, 21 November 2014, www.leparisienne.fr/.../rdc-le-corps-des-femmes-est-un-c....

4 United Nations, Tackling sexual violence must include prevention, ending impunity – UN official, 27 April 2010, un.org/apps/news/story.asp?NewsID=34502 (accessed July 2015).

5 UNFPA, Secretary-General calls attention to scourge of sexual violence in DRC, 1 March 2009, http://www.unfpa.org/public/News/pid/2181 (accessed July 2015).

6 In its report, the UNJHRO clearly states: 'Given the large number of cases of sexual violence ... figures included in the report do not purport to represent the total number of cases of sexual violence in the country', but only those committed by state agents and armed groups; see MONUSCO/UNJHRO, Progress and obstacles in the fight against impunity for

sexual violence in the Democratic Republic of the Congo, April 2014, www.monusco.unmissions.org/LinkClick.aspx? fileticket=Gyh.. (accessed July 2015), 5.

7 These statistics by no means imply that they are regarded as the real/correct numbers of violations committed – they merely serve as an illustration of the magnitude of the problem.

8 MONUSCO/UNJHRO, Progress and obstacles in the fight against impunity for sexual violence in the Democratic Republic of the Congo, April 2014, www.monusco.unmissions.org/LinkClick.aspx?fileticket=Gyh.. (accessed July 2015). In a first effort to systematically compile data on SGBV, the Ministry of Gender (together with the UNPF-United Nations Population Fund) reported 10 685 cases of sexual violence in 2011 and 15 654 in 2012. The study was conducted in 180 of the country's 515 health zones in seven provinces (covering only 35% of Congolese territory); see République Démocratique du Congo, Ministère du Genre, de la Famille et de l'Enfant, *Ampleur des violences sexuelles en RDC et actions de lutte contre le phénomène de 2011 à 2012*, 2013.

9 United Nations Security Council, *Conflict-related sexual violence, report of the Secretary-General* (S/2015/203), 23 March 2015, 9, www.securitycouncilreport.org/atf/cf%7B65BFCF9B...s_2015_203.pdf

10 R Buchanan, More than 100 women raped in brutal mass attack on town in Democratic Republic of Congo, *The Independent*, 15 May 2015, www.independent.co.uk/.../more-than-100-women-raped-in-single-attack-o...; RDC: près de 130 femmes violées selon MSF, *Le figaro*, 15 May 2015, www.lefigar.fr/...2015/.../15/97001-20150515FILW...

11 See, for example, SM Tlapek, Women's status and intimate partner violence in the Democratic Republic of Congo, *Journal of Interpersonal Violence*, 30:14, 2015; M Mulumeoderhwa and G Harris, Forced sex, rape and sexual exploitation: attitudes and experiences of high school students in South Kivu, Democratic Republic of Congo, *Culture, Health and Sex*, 17, 2015.

12 République Démocratique du Congo, Ministère du Genre, de la Famille et de l'Enfant, *Rapport national sur la revue et evaluation du Plan D'Action de Beijing +20*, 2014. See also the figures above recorded by the UNFPA which indicate that 61% of cases of SGBV are not directly related to the dynamics of armed conflict.

13 J Freedman, Explaining sexual violence and gender inequalities in the Democratic Republic of the Congo, *Peace Review*, 23, 2011.

14 E Baaz and M Stern, *The complexity of violence: a critical analysis of sexual violence in the Democratic Republic of Congo*, Uppsala: Nordic Africa Institute, 2010.

15 Ibid. See also J Freedman, Treating sexual violence as a 'business': reflections on national and international responses to sexual and gender-based violence in the Democratic Republic of Congo, in MT Segal and V Demos (eds.), *Gendered perspectives on conflict and violence: part B*, Bingley: Emerald, 2014.

16 Baaz & Stern emphasise the difficulty of getting funding for projects dealing with other forms of violence; see E Baaz and M Stern, *The complexity of violence: a critical analysis of sexual violence in the Democratic Republic of Congo*, Uppsala: Nordic Africa Institute, 2010.

17 J Freedman, Treating sexual violence as a 'business': reflections on national and international responses to sexual and gender-based violence in the Democratic Republic of Congo, in MT Segal and V Demos (eds.), *Gendered perspectives on conflict and violence: part B*, Bingley: Emerald, 2014, 136. Baaz and Stern, and Freedman, elaborate (based on fieldwork in the DRC) on the manner in which 'rape claims' are used to access services (such as health) which are generally not readily accessible; see E Baaz and M Stern, *The complexity of violence: a critical analysis of sexual violence in the Democratic Republic of Congo*, Uppsala: Nordic Africa Institute, 2010; J Freedman, Treating sexual violence as a 'business': reflections on national and international responses to sexual and gender-based violence in the Democratic Republic of Congo, in MT Segal and V Demos (eds.), *Gendered perspectives on conflict and violence: part B*, Bingley: Emerald, 2014.

18 J Freedman, Treating sexual violence as a 'business': reflections on national and international responses to sexual and gender-based violence in the Democratic Republic of Congo, in MT Segal and V Demos (eds.), *Gendered perspectives on conflict and violence: part B*, Bingley: Emerald, 2014.

19 E Baaz and M Stern, *The complexity of violence: a critical analysis of sexual violence in the Democratic Republic of Congo*, Uppsala: Nordic Africa Institute, 2010, 45.

20 G Breton-Le Goff, Ending sexual violence in the Democratic Republic of Congo, *Fletcher Forum of World Affairs*, 34, 2010; J Freedman, Treating sexual violence as a 'business': reflections on national and international responses to sexual and gender-based violence in the Democratic Republic of Congo, in MT Segal and V Demos (eds.), *Gendered perspectives on conflict and violence: part B*, Bingley: Emerald, 2014.

21 See, for example, MONUSCO/United Nations, *Progress and obstacles in the fight against impunity for sexual violence in the Democratic Republic of the Congo*, April 2014, www.monusco.unmissions.org/LinkClick.aspx?fileticket=Gyh.. (accessed July 2015).

22 DP Zonge, The new sexual violence legislation in the Congo: dressing indelible scars on human dignity, *African Studies Review*, 55:2, 2012, 45.

23 République Démocratique du Congo, Ministère du Genre, de la Famille et de l'Enfant, *Rapport national sur la revue et evaluation du Plan D'Action de Beijing +20*, 2014.

24 Congo-Kinshasa: appointed to fight sexual violence and recruitment of child soldiers in the DRC, *AllAfrica*, 28 July 2014, http://allafrica.com/stories/201407290843.html (accessed July 2015).

25 Human Rights Watch, Democratic Republic of Congo: ending impunity for sexual violence, 10 June 2014, www.hrw. org/2014/10 democratic-republic-congo-ending-imp, 3–4. https://www.hrw.org/.../2014.../10/democratic-republic-congo-ending-imp...

26 République Démocratique du Congo, Ministère du Genre, de la Famille et de l'Enfant, *Ampleur des violences sexuelles en RDC et actions de lutte contre le phénomène de 2011 à 2012*, 2013.

27 United Nations Security Council, *Conflict-related sexual violence, report of the Secretary-General* (S/2015/203), 23 March 2015. www.securitycouncilreport.org/atf/cf%7B65BFCF9B...s_2015_203.pdf

28 GNWP, *Security Council Resolution 1325: in-country monitoring report – Democratic Republic of Congo*, 2014, www.gnwp. org/sites/default/.../ICR_2014_DRCongo%207.27.15_0.pdf (accessed July 2015).

29 L Davis, P Fabbri, and IM Alphonse, *Democratic Republic of Congo – DRC: gender country profile 2014*, London: Swedish Embassy, 2014.

30 République Démocratique du Congo, Ministère du Genre, de la Famille et de l'Enfant, *Rapport national sur la revue et evaluation du Plan D'Action de Beijing +20*, 2014, 21–22. For rape trials in civilian criminal courts in the eastern Congo, see also M Lake, Organizing hypocrisy: providing legal accountability for human rights violations in areas of limited statehood, *International Studies Quarterly*, 58, 2014.

31 MONUSCO/United Nations, *Progress and obstacles in the fight against impunity for sexual violence in the Democratic Republic of the Congo*, April 2014, www.monusco.unmissions.org/LinkClick.aspx?fileticket=Gyh.. (accessed July 2015).

32 United Nations Security Council, *Conflict-related sexual violence, report of the Secretary-General* (S/2015/203), 23 March 2015. www.securitycouncilreport.org/atf/cf%7B65BFCF9B...s_2015_203.pdf

33 MONUSCO/United Nations, *Progress and obstacles in the fight against impunity for sexual violence in the Democratic Republic of the Congo*, April 2014, www.monusco.unmissions.org/LinkClick.aspx?fileticket=Gyh.. (accessed July 2015).

34 United Nations Security Council, *Conflict-related sexual violence, report of the Secretary-General* (S/2015/203), 23 March 2015. www.securitycouncilreport.org/atf/cf%7B65BFCF9B...s_2015_203.pdf

35 MONUSCO/United Nations, *Progress and obstacles in the fight against impunity for sexual violence in the Democratic Republic of the Congo*, April 2014, www.monusco.unmissions.org/LinkClick.aspx?fileticket=Gyh.. (accessed July 2015).

36 United Nations, UN, DRC: military pledge marks milestone on road to ending conflict-related sexual violence, press statement by the special representative of the Secretary General on sexual violence in conflict, Zeinab Hawa Bangura, 31 March 2015, www.un.org/.../drc-military-pledgemarks-milestone-on-road-to-ending-co (accessed July 2015).

37 J Guéhenno, DRC – no running away: UN peacekeeping's race against time in DR Congo, 20 July 2015, blog. crisisgroup.org/.../no-running-away-un-peacekeepings-race-against-ti...

38 GNWP, *Security Council Resolution 1325: in-country monitoring report – Democratic Republic of Congo*, 2014, www.gnwp. org/sites/default/.../ICR_2014_DRCongo%207.27.15_0.pdf (accessed July 2015); DRC – follow-up on last month's consultations, *Presidential Power*, 1 November 2013, presidential-power.com/?cat=65. On the initiative of President Kabila, the national consultations resulted in 619 recommendations that he has promised to act on. The consultations brought together 700 participants from political parties and civil society under the leadership of the chairs of the national assembly and senate. Absent from these were armed groups currently active in the east, who were not invited, and leading opposition parties, who refused to participate.

39 GNWP, *Security Council Resolution 1325: in-country monitoring report – Democratic Republic of Congo*, 2014, www.gnwp. org/sites/default/.../ICR_2014_DRCongo%207.27.15_0.pdf (accessed July 2015).

40 E Baaz, Not enough to add women and stir, *Annual Report 2010*, Uppsala: Nordic Africa Institute, 2011, 20–21.

41 GNWP, *Security Council Resolution 1325: in-country monitoring report – Democratic Republic of Congo*, 2014, www.gnwp. org/sites/default/.../ICR_2014_DRCongo%207.27.15_0.pdf (accessed July 2015).

42 RDC, Loi no 87-101-portant Code de la Famille, August 1987, leganet.cd/legislation.htm

43 Parité homme-femme: RDC, les chiffres qui inquiètent, *Digital Congo*, November 2014, www.digitalcongo.net/article/ 103773

44 Y Sadie, Women and peace-building in the Democratic Republic of Congo, *Strategic Review for Southern Africa*, 32, 2010.

Kenya and Somalia

Fragile constitutional gains for women and the threat of patriarchy

Hawa Noor Mohammed

Much research has been done on patriarchy in numerous contexts in Africa, contributing to an understanding of the phenomenon. Recent developments in Kenya and Somalia, characterised by the adoption of new constitutions against the backdrop of stringent patriarchal practices, prompted the writing of this article. Kenya's journey towards gender equality has not been an easy one, given that prior to 2010 – when its new constitution was adopted – customary law that endorsed the violation of women's rights held precedence. For Somalia, over two decades of civil war had encouraged lawlessness, which acted as a barrier for women's progress. With the two countries' new constitutions now in place, expectations are high that past hindrances will be eradicated. Kenya and Somalia stand a good chance of achieving gender equality if lessons from other countries can be carefully considered to avoid a repeat of their failures. Using secondary and primary data, it is this article's argument that an honest dialogue on women's rights involving all relevant stakeholders needs to be initiated to tackle the deeper structural problem of patriarchy, which poses a huge threat to the gains achieved on paper.

Introduction

The struggle for gender equality in Africa broadly, and in Kenya and Somalia in particular, is an ongoing process with many challenges, most of which are related to culture. In Kenya, for instance, the process of domesticating international treaties and conventions – such as the Convention on the Elimination of all Forms of Discrimination against Women (CEDAW) and the African Charter on Human and People's Rights on the Rights of Women in Africa (Maputo Protocol) – to complement national laws has been painstakingly slow. In neighbouring Somalia, the long period of war and the absence of a functional central government have not only restricted progress in women's development but have also resulted in serious violations of women's rights. Like most African countries, both Kenya and Somalia are patriarchal societies. At independence, Kenya's patriarchal practices were embedded in the country's constitution as 'personal/customary law', and this is seen to have contributed to entrenching gender discrimination. Somalia, on the other hand, is perceived as one of the worst places in the world for women to live, particularly because of its strong patriarchal culture.[1]

Both Kenya and Somalia adopted new constitutions in 2010 and 2012 respectively, with seemingly progressive provisions for women's empowerment. Although the new constitutions and related legislative gains seem, on paper, to be positive steps towards enabling women's participation in political and governance processes, there remains a concern around the practical implementation of these legislative gains, especially in the context of dominant patriarchal cultural practices. The issue is compounded by entrenched discriminative cultural practices that have not only assumed religious dimensions but have also coaxed women into embracing the practices they see as culturally and religiously ordained, thus resigning themselves to an 'inferior position' in society. There are also other catalytic factors – such as the failure to include all relevant stakeholders, ineffectiveness and inefficiency of law enforcement institutions, and lack of committed political will – which complicate the processes of promoting women's empowerment in both contexts.

The aim of this article is to analyse selected significant gains for women in the two countries in the context of their newly adopted constitutions, in order to outline achievements and also delineate obstacles to the advancement of gender equality. The article's main argument is that in spite of the reasonable gains in empowering women in both countries, a lot still remains to be done to eliminate various culture-related forms of gender discrimination and challenges to women's emancipation, and that any gains may be undermined if the adverse structural and cultural issues are not addressed.

The article will provide background on gender equality and relevant instruments worldwide before narrowing down in scope to the specific situations in Somalia and Kenya, outlining some contentious issues of customary law that have been prevalent in the debate on gender equality in both countries before and after the adoption of their new constitutions. This will be done in the context of the provisions of CEDAW and the Maputo Protocol. The final section will appraise the nexus between constitutional provisions on paper and the reality in practice in the struggle for gender justice and social equity.

Gender equality in context

Gender equality is a human rights issue that implies equal opportunities for both men and women to realise their full potential and contribute to development without barriers set by stereotypes and socially constructed gender roles. This means that the responsibilities and opportunities of individuals are made and enjoyed irrespective of their sex. Achieving gender equity is premised on putting mechanisms in place to promote fairness in accessing opportunities for all, based on historical injustices faced by women in the past. Fairness means addressing the needs of both sexes in order to level the playing field and may involve 'equal treatment or treatment that is different but which is considered equivalent in terms of rights, benefits, obligations and opportunities'.[2] The debate on gender equality is informed by the need for gender justice.

Mainstream gender activism started with European and American feminist movements in the early 19th century demanding equal rights for women, such as the right to vote, work, have equal pay, own property and experience equality in the family. In Africa, diverse feminist movements drew influence from the international and regional women's rights agencies and emerged strongly to engage in developmental issues during the immediate post-independence period. In the 1990s, the focus was on political activities and the fight for democracy. Today, gender equality is an essential sustainable development and good governance issue, one that emphasises social justice through inclusivity and has taken different shapes and cultural interpretations in order to fit diverse contexts.[3] Positive outcomes have been recorded globally, such as increased numbers of women in political positions, and improved access to education and labour markets, among others, despite numerous backlashes.[4]

Relevant instruments

The increased global struggle for gender equality resulted in the need to put in place mechanisms for safeguarding women's rights and entrenching social justice. A number of international instruments emerged, including the Universal Declaration of Human Rights (UDHR), which contains general non-discrimination clauses on human rights, including that of women, and CEDAW. The latter came about as a result of efforts to have international standards on the rights of men and women in a single document in order to ensure efficiency in their implementation. The United Nations' (UN) Commission on the Status of Women worked to consolidate the various declarations and treaties culminating in CEDAW's adoption by the UN General Assembly in 1979, and it came into force in 1981. Thus far, 185 nations across the globe have ratified CEDAW, with the exception of Somalia, South Sudan, Sudan, the United States (US), Iran, Palau and Tonga.[5] The convention is the most comprehensive document on women's rights, comprising 30 articles; it 'defines what constitutes discrimination against women, and sets up an agenda for national action to end such discrimination'.[6] It also addresses customs and traditions vis-à-vis the rights of rural women.

The Beijing Platform for Action supports the principles of CEDAW and previous resolutions for the advancement of women's rights. It was the outcome of the 1995 Fourth World Conference on Women held in Beijing, China, which echoed earlier commitments towards gender justice and prescribed more roles for various stakeholders, including governments, the international community, non-governmental organisations (NGOs) and the private sector.[7] In essence, 12 critical areas of concern that shape intervention strategies are pointed out in the Beijing Platform for Action, namely poverty, education and training, health, violence against women, armed conflict, economy, power and decision-making, institutional mechanisms for the advancement of women, human rights, the media, the environment, and the girl-child.[8] Regional bodies as well as individual states are required to domesticate these emphasised areas.

CEDAW and the Beijing Platform for Action are the main international treaties aimed at righting gender inequality, although there are other international instruments relevant to this article worth mentioning: the Optional Protocol to CEDAW (2000), the Convention on Consent to Marriage, Minimum Age for Marriage and Registration of Marriage (1964), the Convention on the Nationality of Married Women (1958), the Convention on the Political Rights of Women (1954), the Declaration on the Elimination of Violence against Women (1993), the Commission on Human Rights Resolution on Land Ownership (2003/22), the Declaration on the Protection of Women and Children in Emergency and Armed Conflict (1974) and UN Security Council (UNSC) Resolution 1325 (2000).[9]

In Africa, there are a number of instruments besides CEDAW, namely the Protocol to the African Charter on Human and People's Rights on the Rights of Women in Africa (also known as the Maputo Protocol), the African Union (AU) Solemn Declaration on Gender Equality in Africa, and the AU Gender Policy, among other sub-regional treaties and national instruments. The Maputo Protocol was adopted in 2003 in Maputo, Mozambique, and was aimed at addressing African women's rights within the African context. It is the most comprehensive regional women's rights instrument, which complements CEDAW to guarantee women's rights. The ratification of an international treaty translates into an acceptance by the ratifying state to domesticate the international treaty in its national laws; being a signatory means that a state is under an obligation not to contradict the provisions of that international treaty. Entering reservations means that a country purports to exclude certain provisions of the treaty and their application within its territory. This is often informed by a conflict of interest between provisions in a treaty, national laws and common, local, cultural and religious practices, as is the case with the Maputo Protocol, which was opposed by some civil society groups that claimed that some of its provisions contradict their religious beliefs and undermine the African culture.[10]

These documents provide substantial legislative and policy framework to deal with gender equity and equality issues, both at the global and continental level; as such, continued gender inequality cannot be blamed on a shortage of such instruments.

Kenya and Somalia

Kenya and Somalia are neighbouring countries that have plenty in common, including the simultaneous adoption of new constitutions within the same period. The large north-eastern region of Kenya is occupied by the Somali ethnic group and so cultures across the borders are similar. The societal structure in both countries, like many others in Africa, is patriarchal in nature, although their different histories have led to varying degrees of these practices. While Kenya is a heterogeneous society with 42 coexisting ethnic groups (one of them being the Somali), Somalia is homogeneous with the Somali being the main ethnic group – the only existing subgroups are the numerous clans that emanate from one Somali 'family'. Various religions, among them Christianity and Islam, are practised in Kenya, while Islam is the predominant religion in Somalia. As a bordering country, Kenya has spearheaded the Somali peace processes, including hosting and supporting mediation and various Somali administrations, including the 2004 transitional federal government and the current government. In this regard, Kenya has portrayed itself as an experienced 'big brother' to be emulated; however, since Kenya's defence forces were deployed in Somalia in 2011, some factions in Somalia see Kenya as an enemy driven by its own national interests.

In both Kenya and Somalia, women's contribution towards development has been significant. In terms of progress on gender equality, Somalia lags behind Kenya due to its prolonged conflict and the lack of a functioning government to guarantee its citizens' human rights. Kenya, on the other hand, has enjoyed relative stability and so the struggle for gender equality, although not yet fully achieved, is relatively more progressive. Kenya has ratified CEDAW[11] and has signed and ratified the Maputo Protocol, albeit with reservations relating to customary law,[12] while Somalia is one of the few countries that has neither signed nor ratified CEDAW but is a signatory to the Maputo Protocol.

In Kenya, women have always played an active role in managing land, a fundamental source of livelihood in the African context. With the emergence of colonialism, however, women lost their land, translating to a loss of freedom – and this forced them to depend on men for their livelihood, contrary to the pre-colonial period, when most communities were ruled by councils of elders and women acted as farm managers. Their dependence on men thus generated conducive grounds for patriarchy and male domination that continued over the years and beyond independence in 1963.[13] In Kenya, women's active participation was demonstrated in the anti-colonial struggle of the 1950s and 1960s, as child bearers, caretakers and providers for the family and society in the domestic sphere and by sheltering, feeding and arming freedom fighters, as well as acting as combatants in the public sphere. Besides this, women's status was also defined through cultural practices such as female genital mutilation (FGM) and customary law, both of which were common practice in most African societies, including Kenya, prior to colonisation.[14]

The constitution Kenya adopted at independence in 1963 borrowed from local customs on issues of gender and included provisions on 'customary/personal laws' that were used to inform the interpretation of matters. This is particularly evident with Section 82(4), which makes reference to personal/customary laws in the regulation of family matters such as marriage, adoption, divorce and inheritance.[15] Today, in the majority of Kenya's 42 ethnic groups, the role of women is still defined by culture and religion. Informal separate spheres for men and women exist and, as a result, the country's record on issues of women's rights is mixed. The incompatibility of customary practices with international women's rights standards has thus been a stumbling block to the realisation of women's rights in Kenya.

Somalia has never enacted any gender-related legislation or policies, but this can partly be explained by the prolonged period of civil war that adversely affected the country.[16] More than two decades of civil war, marked by the collapse of the central government, meant that the structures that protected human rights were destroyed, causing devastation and suffering among Somalia's vulnerable populations.

The country's history, however, shows that since the advent of urbanisation at the end of the Second World War, women have played fundamental roles in society, albeit in often informal and unrecognised ways, such as through sewing, weaving, embroidery, etc.[17] These roles widened further under the military regime of the 1970s and 1980s, marked by increased school enrolment and job opportunities in institutions such as the army.[18] The migration of many Somali men to the Gulf states in the mid 1970s for better employment and other opportunities led to increased responsibilities for the women who were left behind. The flipside, however, was that when the men returned they brought with them new calls for the re-Islamisation of Somali society, with the aim of curbing the Western secular influence at the time.[19] This has had a huge impact on the status of women because it has constrained their visibility in the public sphere, manifested through violence such as rape, clan-related reprisals and murder through public stoning, maternal mortality, FGM, discrimination under customary laws, and the demand to fulfil stipulated responsibilities. This has resulted in women being torn between inflexible cultural values that work to their disadvantage and their own attempts to participate in nation-building activities.

A strong traditional clan system (known as *beel*) is informally used to regulate most social affairs and deliberations in the Somali homogenous culture,[20] where male clan leaders have powers to decide on various aspects of the Somali social lifestyle, lineage issues, and conflict resolution.[21] As the majority of Somalis are Muslim, both Islam and the local traditional pastoralist culture pillared in clan membership are applicable. In spite of this, Somali women have remained resilient by lobbying clan elites to prioritise peace during clan conflict-resolution gatherings, in which women do not traditionally participate, mobilising women's peace lobby groups, and providing shelter, medical care, food and medication to combatants, as well as taking care of their families.[22]

In the past three years, there have been important developments in Somalia, including the adoption of a provisional constitution before the country's 2012 elections, which led to the establishment of the Federal Government of Somalia (FGS) under President Hassan Sheikh Mahmoud. The progressive provisional constitution (to be voted for in a referendum by 2016) was overwhelmingly voted for by delegates at the National Constituent Assembly (NCA),[23] and is founded on Islamic Shari'ah law.[24] This means that Shari'ah and national laws must conform to it. The founding principles of the constitution are the basis for protecting human rights in Somalia, and aim to include women in all spheres of national development.[25]

The next section looks at selected contentious issues in the debate on women's empowerment in Kenya and Somalia before the adoption of their respective constitutions and the gains made. There is a focus on matters related to customary laws, which are critical to any discussion on women's rights because the home environment is where these laws mostly apply, and where they are also most susceptible to violation. It is therefore assumed that if women's rights (and other rights in general) are respected within the smaller home and community circles, it is highly likely that this will be replicated in the national and other broader spheres.

Issues of customary law

Discrimination against women is defined in CEDAW's Article 1 as

> any distinction, exclusion or restriction made on the basis of sex which has the effect or purpose of impairing or nullifying the recognition, enjoyment or exercise by women, irrespective of their marital status, on a basis of equality of men and women, of human rights and fundamental freedoms in the political, economic, social, cultural, civil or any other field.[26]

States parties are thus required to 'condemn discrimination against women in all its forms and agree to pursue by all appropriate means and without delay a policy of eliminating discrimination, with mechanisms through law and other means to eliminate any kind of discrimination' by including the principles of gender equality in respective national legislations.[27]

There were various contradictions between Kenya's domestic laws and the two international instruments referred to above – CEDAW and the Maputo Protocol. While the Independence Constitution contained a number of non-discrimination principles, these principles were often reversed by other clauses that recognised customary law. For instance, Section 82(1) and 82(3) of the Independence Constitution guaranteed fundamental rights and freedoms for all without discrimination, including sex-based discrimination.[28] Interestingly, however, Section 82(4) abrogated the above by recognising the unwritten personal laws based on customs and/or religion.[29] Sources of these personal laws are: the African customary law of the various customary groups; the Hindu Marriage and Divorce Act (Laws of Kenya, Chapter 157) based on Hindu law and governing adherence of the Hindu faith; the Mohammedan Marriage and Divorce Act (Laws of Kenya, Chapter 156) based on Islamic law and governing adherence to the Islamic faith; and the Marriage Act (Laws of Kenya, Chapter 150) and African Christian Marriage and Divorce Act (Laws of Kenya, Chapter 151), applying to people who have chosen to 'marry under the formal law, regardless of their cultural or religious practices'.[30] These personal laws were left open to interpretation – but in a society where cultures and traditions are generally in favour of men, this meant that women's rights, especially in the domestic sphere, were prone to subjugation.[31]

Attempts to reform family law in Kenya started as early as 1967 when two commissions were appointed by then-president Jomo Kenyatta to review the laws on marriage, divorce and succession, and integrate them into a single document.[32] Only succession laws were legislated, while three attempts to pass a bill on marriage and divorce were defeated on the grounds that they were offensive to local customs and that women did not deserve to have 'too many rights'.[33] Further attempts at this were equally unsuccessful.

Today, Kenya's 2010 constitution records some gains for women aimed at guaranteeing freedom from discrimination for them and other marginalised groups. What constitutes discrimination is elaborated in Article 27.[34] Discrimination in matters of 'personal law' has been abolished by excluding the provisions of Article 82(4) of the independence constitution from the 2010 constitution. The only such exception is in the application of Muslim law (laws derived from the teachings of Islam), which equally comes with strict limitations to avoid patriarchal interpretations, as stated in Article 24(4) of the 2010 constitution.[35] Flexibility is equally guaranteed for those who opt for it,[36] with an emphasis on the supremacy of the 2010 constitution of Kenya over and above customary and personal laws.[37]

Universal marriage registration and the minimum age for marriage are also addressed in the 2010 constitution, including a framework for further legislation whereby Parliament was required to enact laws recognising marriage systems based on religion and custom so that a system to regulate such marriages through documentation exists.[38] Consequent upon this, the new Marriage Act was passed in April 2014. Even though criticised for a number of shortcomings,[39] the act contains significant gains, such as a stipulation for the minimum age for marriage to be 18 years across all cultural groups, as well as the requirement that all marriages be registered, including those performed under customary law. As a result, women – especially those who historically have been denied their rights under customary law, such as that of inheritance by family members of a deceased husband – can now legitimately launch claims using their customary marriage registration documents. The requirement for the registration of all marriages also allows for the protection of dependents and spouse(s) of deceased persons, as opposed to the provisions of the previous Law of Succession Act of 1981, which required widows but not widowers to give up their interest in the deceased's property upon remarrying. Also, all pre-existing laws relating to marriage have now been incorporated into a single document under the act, with each marriage partner having equal legal status, as well as equal parental responsibility to ensure that single parents, especially mothers, do not carry the burden of childcare on their own.[40] The new act legalises polygamy in customary and Islamic marriages so that a man can marry as many women as he pleases without the consent of the first wife. It is noteworthy that during the debating of the Marriage Bill, male legislators voted in unity despite their usual party divisions, forcing female legislators, frustrated by their minimal number, to march out of Parliament in protest. As a result, the bill became law. It remains to be seen how well the act will regulate the marriage institution in Kenya.

Parliament was also required to enact legislation within five years to regulate matrimonial property during and at the end of a marriage.[41] Article 40(2) of the 2010 constitution on the right to property prevents Parliament from enacting any law that will permit the state or any other person to deprive another of property on discriminatory grounds. It is highly commendable that the Matrimonial Property Act of 2013, which clearly defines what constitutes matrimonial property and stipulates procedures for its regulation, is already in place. Although the tabling of this act initially elicited sharp division among legislators, the new act defines matrimonial property as home, households and 'effects in the matrimonial home; movable or immovable property owned by both or either spouse and acquired during the subsistence of the marriage, or any other property acquired during the subsistence of the marriage only'.[42] This means that property acquired before a marriage does not amount to matrimonial property. Both spouses have equal rights to own property and enter into contracts, as well as equal rights in matrimonial property and liabilities at the time of marriage, during the marriage and separation, regardless of contribution by either party. Contribution is defined as both monetary and non-monetary, including domestic work, management of the matrimonial home, childcare, companionship, and management of family business or property and farm work. This, together with the allocation of such property, is, however, to be defined by a court of law.[43] Similarly, the recognition of polygamous unions in the new Marriage Act comes with the caution that property acquired before marriage to a second wife belongs to the man and the first wife, while that acquired after marriage to a second wife belongs to the three parties to the marriage and so on, depending on the number of women in the union.[44] The system used during marriage (including customary) is to be used in the division of matrimonial property, but this also comes with the requirement that the application should be in line with the 2010 constitution. The new Matrimonial Property Act also protects spouses from the sale of matrimonial property without the knowledge of the other,[45] complementing the fact that a party to a marriage can now file a suit to determine a share in matrimonial property without filing for divorce, whereas the eviction of a spouse by third parties is prohibited unless a court order is obtained. Despite its imperfections, a major gain of the Matrimonial Property Act of 2013 is the fact that there now exists comprehensive legislation to regulate matrimonial property, particularly in Kenya's context where properties have mostly borne the man's name, meaning women have lost out when a marriage comes to an end or upon the death of a spouse.

In case of the need to address these matters in a court of law, Article 48 of the 2010 constitution guarantees access to justice for all without discrimination and is in harmony with CEDAW and the Maputo Protocol.[46] Similarly, the dignity of every person and the right to have that dignity respected, and the right of every person to freedom and security, including freedom from any kind of torture and punishment, are emphasised in Articles 28 and 29.[47] This could imply harmful 'customary practices such as spousal beating (chastisement), female genital surgeries and widow inheritance that can now be challenged on constitutional grounds'.[48] Women are now also recognised among vulnerable groups whose needs should be addressed by the state and public offices.[49]

For Somalia, chapter two of the new provisional constitution, similar to the Transitional Charter, provides for the fundamental rights and duties of the citizen and guarantees equality and non-discrimination for all. Article 1 calls for non-discrimination and the equality of all citizens, stating that it is the duty of the state as well as responsible institutions to uphold the principle of non-discrimination.[50] Women have also been accorded special rights to protection from discrimination in the workplace,[51] a guarantee of support to realise their socio-economic rights, and an affirmation of the inviolability of human dignity, including that of women.[52] Article 40 sets out considerations for the interpretation of these fundamental rights and states that rights can be interpreted in terms of international law, Shari'ah and the decision of courts in other countries.[53] This article also recognises customary law as long as it conforms to Shari'ah law and the constitution.

Article 28 defines marriage as the foundation of society and goes further to state that the consent of both parties, one or both of whom must have reached the age of 'maturity', must be sought before a marriage transaction can be contracted.[54] The term 'maturity' in this case is open to interpretation, but Article 29(8) defines a child as anybody below the age of 18 years.[55] Although it is clear that marriage can only be contracted with the full consent of both parties, the demand for having reached the age of 'maturity' of at 'least one marriage party' is a grey area that requires further legislation for the sake of protecting children. The term 'maturity' particularly needs further clarity to avoid misinterpretation. In this context, it is important to highlight that marriage within specific clans/bloodlines is encouraged in Somali culture, and society has the power to exercise authority in identifying suitable matches, sometimes without the potential couple's consent.[56] In cases where one (usually the woman) or both of the identified pair resist clan elders can use the threat of a curse to compel them to abide; and in a context where legislation is not clear, this poses a major challenge.[57]

FGM is prohibited through Article 15 on the right to security and liberty of every person and freedom from violence.[58] In this article, FGM is described as 'a cruel and degrading customary practice, and is tantamount to torture'. Article 31(1) speaks to the issue of harmful cultural practices, affirming that the state will protect the culture of the Somali people while at the same time eliminating harmful cultural practices.[59] The cultural practices referred to here could imply any practice, such as FGM and wife inheritance, that has negative effects on the well-being of the society as a whole. Controversy does arise, however, around who determines what is harmful and what is not, and whether women have the power to decide what they consider to be harmful. According to the estimates of the World Health Organization (WHO), between 100 and 140 million girls and women worldwide have undergone different forms of FGM. In Somalia, the FGM rate stands at 98%, with 80–90% of women having had a part or all of their genitalia removed and stitched together.[60] A victim's consent is seldom sought before FGM is performed, so FGM is considered a form of gender-based violence with huge negative impacts on health, which can result in death.[61] Most communities that condone FGM believe that by undergoing the practice a girl becomes mature and ready to have her own family, while at the same time providing an opportunity for society to gain wealth in the form of dowry. The practice is believed to protect a girl's chastity, which is an honour to the family/clan/society. Investing in a girl's education is often not emphasised in Somali custom, as it is widely believed that she will eventually leave her family to join another after marriage. This is solidified by the belief that a woman does not naturally have an ethnic group and so investing in her is pointless.

Another form of harmful cultural practice acceptable in Somali culture, which could be implied in the above-mentioned article, is wife inheritance (*dumaal*). In this practice, a brother or any other relative of a woman's deceased husband marries her after the death of her spouse, while a man can marry a sister of his deceased wife (*xigsiisan*).[62] The rationale behind this practice is to ensure that child care and wealth is retained within the same extended family. Elsewhere, such as Kenya, the practice has been criticised for its contribution to increased rates of HIV/AIDS, as well as robbing women of their dignity and the right to determine their destiny by commoditising them and treating them as property.

Political participation and decision-making

In the public and political spheres, the need to involve women as equal stakeholders is underscored in CEDAW's Article 7, which requires that states parties

> eliminate discrimination against women in political and public life so that they can participate in voting in all elections and referenda, be eligible for election and participate in policy formulation and implementation, including holding of public office at all levels of government.[63]

This is echoed in Article 9 of the Maputo Protocol, which requires states parties to take affirmative measures in order to promote the equal participation of women in national politics, as well as in elections and electoral processes. It also urges for women's equal participation in all governance and development levels, including decision-making and policy development.[64]

The reality for Kenyan women before the promulgation of the 2010 constitution was gloomy. Despite their hard work, women remained marginalised and excluded from decision-making on crucial issues, especially those that affected them and in which they should naturally have had a voice. The fact that there existed no legal guiding principle to promote gender equality in political parties prior to 2010, coupled with gender stereotyping, was a huge obstacle to their increased participation. It is therefore less surprising that many women still continue to shy away from political involvement, as they would rather maintain 'peace' in the comfort zones of their conventional careers and homes than experience public humiliation, particularly during electoral campaigns. Section 33 of the old constitution on the procedure for filling up the seats for nominated members of Parliament only 'encouraged' political parties to be gender sensitive.[65] Similarly, the 2007 Political Parties Act – the first in the country's history to regulate the activities of political parties – only pointed out the obligation to include one-third of either gender in political parties' national leadership before they could be registered, although holding a position in a political party's national leadership did not guarantee nomination to run for a political office. Such a stipulation without a strategy for checking its adherence gave no assurance that women would hold political positions and, as a result, their numbers remained minimal.[66]

With the new constitution in place, significant strides have been made to ensure that women play an active role in politics and national leadership, such as directing Parliament to enact laws ensuring not more than two-thirds representation of either gender in elective and appointive positions. The adoption of affirmative action is a positive move towards promoting equal opportunity for all and ensuring the participation of marginalised groups (including women), although it had its shortcomings in implementation during the 2013 presidential elections.[67] This was as a result of the 2012 Supreme Court's ruling that the two-thirds gender rule could only be implemented progressively until the year 2015 due to the envisaged practical challenges and the risk of a constitutional crisis.[68] As things now stand, although the gains are a huge contrast compared to the pre-2010-constitution period, the number of women in ministerial and other public appointments remains minimal. Political party politics, as opposed to strategising on the best method for implementing affirmative action, has also taken preference among both male and female legislators. There also exists no clear-cut mechanism for checks and balances on performance, so the actual meaning of 'progressively till the year 2015' remains a grey area.

Other progressive provisions are found in Articles 90(1) and 90(2)(b) of the 2010 constitution, which provide for proportional representation based on party lists, requiring them to alternate between male and female qualified candidates in nominative positions, as well as emphasising the need to uphold the spirit of equality and equity.[69] The Independent Electoral and Boundaries Commission (IEBC) is also urged, among other things, to comply with the principle of gender equality.[70] New provisions emphasising gender equality also exist in other sectors of governance, such as Article 127 (on the Parliamentary Service Commission), Article 232 (on public service), Article 250 (on commissions and independent offices), Article 171 (on the Judicial Service Commission), and Articles 175, 177 and 197 (on devolved government), among others.

The Senate Assembly now includes 16 women nominated on the basis of political party strength, in addition to two slots for the youth and two for persons with disabilities, of which none should be of the same gender.[71] In the National Assembly there are 290 elected members of Parliament, 47 women representatives and 12 nominated members (based on each political party's strength in Parliament), making a total of 349. Women's composition include 12 elected in open contests with men (for the 290 positions), 47 elected on special representative seats (women representatives) reserved for women as a result of affirmative action,[72] and those nominated in the 12 seats set aside for special interest groups, namely the youth, persons with disabilities and workers, which must alternate between male and female candidates. Although every citizen is free to contest any position besides the special ones set aside for special groups, it is significant to point out that only a handful of women were elected in the openly contested National Assembly positions, and none was elected both to the senate and to the 47 county gubernatorial positions – both being key political and decision-making positions in the country.

With the legislative and decision-making levels dominated by men, it is plausible that issues, particularly those that affect women, are still likely to be sabotaged by the male majority based on numerical strength, as witnessed during the enactment of the Marriage Bill 2014 when female legislators walked out in protest as their majority male counterparts united to pass it. This is, however, not to underestimate the efforts of the few male legislators who have been at the forefront of championing for women's rights. Aside from numbers, the unclear delineation of roles and mandates between members of Parliament and women representatives poses another problem; some women representatives have mistaken their responsibilities as being that of representing the entire respective counties, but in reality the essence of women representative positions is to represent the interests of women in the National Assembly. Overall, it is fair to say that the engagement of Kenyan women in politics has remained marginalised, despite the fact that the country is party to various international human rights instruments.

Under the 2004 Transitional Federal Charter (TFC), only 12% of parliamentary positions in Somalia were reserved for women. In 2012, before the adoption of the provisional constitution, stakeholders in the constitution-making process recommended affirmative action in the Somali and International Leaders' National Consultative Constitutional Conference held in Garowe, Puntland in February 2012 to ensure that 30% of the NCA positions were occupied by women (Garowe II principles). This was later also to be included in the provisional constitution, but neither happened. As a result, only 14% of the total numbers of members of Parliament are women, as opposed to the stipulated 30%, and only 20% of cabinet members (in the first cabinet) are women.[73] In the new arrangement, the lower house (house of the people) is elected directly by the people (supposedly representing the entire Somali community) and is comprised of 275 members, while the upper house is comprised of 54 members.

Although Article 133 allows for an amendment that could foresee the 30% quota included, the lack of adherence at such an initial stage gives less hope for the future.[74] The founding principles of the constitution call for the inclusion of women in elected and all national appointments across the three branches of government, including in independent commissions, with existing limitations as long as they are justified by law.[75] As a reflection of deep-rooted gender insensitivity, only one woman was nominated as commissioner in the recently approved list of nominees for the Independent Constitutional Review and Implementation Commission (ICRIC).

Laws to regulate political parties and those on election regulation are yet to be enacted and the steps taken so far, although still fragile, can be seen as gains given the limited role in political participation that women played in the past.

Gender equality for Kenyan and Somali women – are gains on paper a guarantee?

Against the backdrop of decades of campaigning for gender equality, a lingering question is why it should still be a subject of debate. For Somalia, it may be argued that the country's more than two decades of civil war has been a huge hindrance, but the role that women played during the prolonged conflict should not be underestimated.[76] Recently adopted constitutions in Kenya and Somalia with gains for women are now in place, signifying hope for the future, but the implementation of the newly acquired rights remains a huge concern – especially considering the existence of structural patriarchy that has shaped and continues to shape the definition and day-to-day position of women in the two countries.

Patriarchy is a widespread ideology, defined as 'the manifestation and institutionalization of male dominance over women in the society',[77] which has long been justified in using culture and religion to stipulate gender roles.[78] In a patriarchal culture, an individual is socialised to act in defined ways according to societal expectations, where the man is seen as the provider and the woman as the homemaker.[79] Administered through unwritten norms, socialisation starts in the family, where women are obliged to obey and depend on men, and so it is the man who 'appropriates all social roles and keeps women in subordinate positions'.[80] In some contexts, the strength of patriarchy even surpasses religion and is deep rooted among its adherents as members of particular communities collectively strive to maintain cultural practices to prevent erosion and external influence.[81] Whereas cultural practices are positive in the way they define a society's standing, those that are harmful and violate human rights have huge implications for individual and societal well-being. Not only do these patriarchal practices constrain and negatively impact on women but they also put unnecessary burdens and pressure on men.

In Kenya, the prolonged use of the discriminative 'personal law' to regulate marriage, divorce and inheritance – despite the country's having ratified international women's rights treaties – serves to demonstrate the problem of disharmony between deep-rooted unwritten norms that have guarded societal lifestyles for centuries and newer legal frameworks aimed at securing human rights. Discarding these personal laws in Kenya's 2010 constitution and the enactment of two important laws on marriage and matrimonial property, however, are efforts aimed at achieving gender equality and ensuring women are not discriminated against on the basis of culture. The new legislations were driven by the need to curb negative, deep-rooted cultural practices such as wife inheritance, widow's loss of inheritance and matrimonial property, child marriages, parental irresponsibility and gender inequality in accessing justice. Additionally, the adoption of affirmative action to integrate women into positions of power and decision-making was driven by the hope that their increased numbers would translate into the visibility of their abilities and good leadership qualities,[82] and the promotion of their interests, and so be an encouragement for others to follow in their path.

Similarly, Somalia's determination to achieve gender equality is indicated, among other initiatives, by the outlawing of harmful cultural practices such as FGM and wife inheritance, and the need to have more women in decision-making positions. However, despite these efforts, some questions arise regarding the effectiveness of the newly acquired laws in curbing the mentioned cultural obstacles for women. Are laws on paper effective in solving deep structural problems? What happens in situations where the general interpretation of these laws contradicts the spirit of gender equality? And does increased numbers of women in decision-making positions translate proportionally into improvements in women's status and lived reality?

The popularity of gender quotas has led to countries such as Rwanda, Costa Rica, Argentina, Mozambique and South Africa ranking high in the Inter-Parliamentary Union for their significant female political representation, even surpassing the Nordic countries of Denmark, Iceland, Finland, Norway and Sweden that have been high in the global ranking since the 1970s.[83] A critical audit, however, suggested that increased numbers may not necessarily translate to an automatic realisation of gender equality if improperly implemented.[84] The case of South Africa particularly stands out, given the backlash against gender equality witnessed in recent years, in contrast with its experience of having high numbers of women in both government and ministerial positions coupled with its progressive democratic constitution.

During the apartheid era, South African women faced varying degrees of race- and gender-based discrimination, with the worst forms having been imposed upon black women through the Administration Act (1927).[85] As a result, the post-apartheid African National Congress (ANC) regime undertook to protect women through various provisions and a strong legal framework, including Section 9(3) of the constitution, which obligates the state to abolish discrimination and inequality,[86] the Promotion of Equality and Prevention of Unfair Discrimination Act (2000), the Prevention of Domestic Violence Act (1998), and the Recognition of Customary Marriages Act (1998) (to protect women in polygamous unions). A national gender machinery was created; yet despite these efforts, the country is still grappling with issues of gender inequality, with claims that rural women have not reaped the benefits of empowerment. Although women have been accorded special rights, such as those on inheritance and within the family, these rights remain contested in relation to customary courts and in access to communal land, centred on traditional male power over land. Rape and domestic violence is also still rampant in South Africa, among other women's rights violations. As Andrews argues, it is a reflection of the masculine nature of the society rooted in three main waves of patriarchy, namely the authoritarian apartheid state; cultural remnants of a violent anti-apartheid struggle; and indigenous customary law that regards women as minors.[87] South Africa's case seems to resonate with the much-praised Rwanda, whereby, despite women parliamentarians' efforts in transforming the situation of women, there persists a gross mismatch between increased numbers of women in Parliament and the real empowerment of ordinary women at the grassroots.[88]

The lesson therefore that a country such as South Africa offers is that while the increased number of women in decision-making positions is no doubt a positive move aimed at uplifting their status, it is not necessarily the only means to the end. Besides numbers, loyalty and dedication to promoting women's interests against all odds need to be prioritised. Given their new progressive constitutions (at least on paper), Kenya and Somalia stand a high chance of achieving gender equality if lessons from these experienced countries can be carefully considered in order to avoid a repeat of their failures.

What should drive the agenda above all is an appreciation of the existence of deep-rooted cultural norms, practised informally regardless of the legislation in place. It is also important to have a creative strategy among women politicians to balance party politics and prioritising the women's empowerment agenda. It is only through competence, as opposed to nominative and appointive positions, that women can earn respect as good leaders. More and more women in these two countries should join political parties, while those in high-level positions should own the responsibility to support fellow women so as to increase collective strength when it comes to voting, particularly on controversial gender issues. In Somalia, such a strategy will eliminate dependence on clan elders to select them for such positions since, as already evidenced, the exclusion of the 30% gender quota for women in the provisional constitution is an indication of nominal interest in involving women in leadership. The emergence of some factions, such as the Supreme Religious Council (SRC), which argue that Islamic teachings allow women to occupy deputy positions only, while others condemn any participation of women by saying that integrating 'anti-Islamic' aspects in the provisional constitution (i.e., the holding of offices by women, ban on FGM, among others) was an attempt to destroy Islam,[89] is more evidence of their insatiable determination to suppress women.

The problem of patriarchy, being an ideological one, requires dialogue and increased awareness – and the time is ripe for stakeholders in the two countries to open Pandora's box and initiate an honest discussion on women's rights in the context of religion and culture. While doing this, strong caution should be exercised based on the negative image associated with gender rights activism, which portrays women as 'divorcees with scores to settle against men in general'. Awareness raising will be even more effective if the mass media, through sponsored programmes, can be strategically utilised to promote messages against harmful patriarchal practices and popularise the idea that the debate on gender equality is not solely aimed at challenging the man's position but a common good that is, in the end, of benefit to society at large.[90] Women leaders will also need to work closely with media practitioners to challenge stereotypical narratives about them and ensure that their success stories are given wide coverage, with the aim of changing perceptions about women leaders from helpless victims to serious performers.[91]

Given the length of time that Kenya took to change its laws, Somalia should learn from this lesson and avoid following the same trend by utilising the current reconstruction opportunity to fearlessly dive straight into real matters of gender equality and inclusivity. This way, women will also be rewarded for their efforts during the prolonged war. At the same time, the country should work towards the ratification of significant international women's rights treaties, key among them being CEDAW and the Maputo Protocol. Overall, there is need for a thorough and coordinated multi-stakeholder intervention. Above all, religious and cultural leaders as well as law enforcement agencies must ensure that the constitutional gains in the two countries are not swept under the carpet but are fully utilised to benefit women.

Conclusion

Although the new constitutions of Kenya and Somalia present brighter prospects, it is evident that there exist more structural issues to be tackled beyond the gains on paper for the empowerment of women to be fully realised. The relevant provisions in the constitutions of the two countries are, nevertheless, progressive and indeed important contributions in advancing the course of the empowerment of women.

Notes

1 A Albadri, The worst place in the world for women: Somalia, *The Guardian*, 14 June 2011, www.theguardian.com/world/2011/jun/14/worst-places-in-the-world-for-women-somalia

2 UNESCO, Gender equality and equity: a summary review of UNESCO's accomplishments since the Fourth World Conference on Women, 2005, 5, http://unesdoc.unesco.org/images/0012/001211/121145e.pdf, (accessed August 2015).

3 UNESCO, Gender equality in education: what is gender and why is it so important?, www.unescobkk.org/education/gender/what-is-gender-equality/, (accessed August 2015).

4 J Squires, *The new politics of gender equality*, New York, NY: Palgrave Macmillan, 2007.

5 G Mutume, Battling for equality on all fronts: some progress since Beijing, but hurdles persist, *Africa Renewal Online*, 2012, www.un.org/africarenewal/magazine/special-edition-women-2012/battling-equality-all-fronts, (accessed August 2015).

6 UN Women, Convention on the Elimination of all Forms of Discrimination against Women: text of the convention, www.un.org/womenwatch/daw/cedaw/cedaw.htm, (accessed August 2015).

7 UN, Commission on the Status of Women, 49th Session, 29 February–11 March 2005, www.un.org/en/development/devagenda/gender.shtml, (accessed August 2015).

8 UN Women, Fourth World Conference on Women, www.un.org/womenwatch/daw/beijing/platform/, (accessed August 2015).

9 UNESCO, Learning to live together: international standard-setting instruments on women's rights, www.unesco.org/new/en/social-and-human-sciences/themes/gender-equality/legal-instruments/international-legal-instruments, (accessed August 2015).

10 R Gawaya and R Mukasa, The African women's protocol: a new dimension for women's rights in Africa, *Gender and Development*, 13:3, 2005.

11 M Celestine, *Promoting the human rights of women in Kenya: a comparative review of the domestic laws*, Kenya, Nairobi: UNIFEM, 2010.

12 Make Every Woman Count, Promoting the empowerment of African women and girls, Africa: Maputo Protocol, 28 May 2011, www.makeeverywomancount.org/index.php?option=com_content&id=892:africa-maputo-protocol&Itemid=146, (accessed August 2015).

13 Institute for Economic Affairs, Profiles of women's socio-economic status in Kenya, June 2008, http://ke.boell.org/sites/default/files/profile_of_womens_socio-economic_status_in_kenya_1.pdf, (accessed August 2015).

14 CG Kariuki, Women's participation in the Kenyan Society, *The African Executive*, 22–28 December 2010, http://africanexecutive.com/downloads/Women's%20participation%20in%20Kenyan%20Society.pdf, (accessed August 2015).

15 M Celestine, *Promoting the human rights of women in Kenya: a comparative review of the domestic laws*, Kenya, Nairobi: UNIFEM, 2010.

16 UNDP, Gender in Somalia, www.undp.org/content/dam/rbas/doc/Women's%20Empowerment/Gender_Somalia.pdf, (accessed August 2015).

17 S Nakaya, Women and gender equality in peace processes: from women at the negotiating table to postwar structural reforms in Guatemala and Somalia, *Global Governance*, 9, 2003.

18 C Abdi, Convergence of civil war and the religious right: reimagining Somali women, *Signs: Journal of Women in Culture and Society*, 33, 2007.

19 UNICEF, Women's rights in Islam and Somali culture, December 2002, www.unicef.org/somalia/SOM_WomenInIslam.pdf, (accessed August 2015).

20 Ibid.

21 F Ssereo, Clan politics, clan-democracy and conflict regulation in Africa: the experience of Somalia, *The Global Review of Ethnopolitics*, 2:3/4, 2003.

22 H Ingiriis & M Hoehne, The impact of civil war and state collapse on the roles of Somali women: a blessing in disguise, *Journal of Eastern African Studies*, 7, 2013.

23 UN officials welcome historic approval of new constitution for Somalia, *UN News Centre*, 1 August 2012, www.un.org/apps/news/story.asp?NewsID=42603#.Vd8MGbCUcrO

24 Provisional Constitution of the Federal Republic of Somalia, Article 3(1): United Nations Political Officer of Somalia (UNPOS).

25 Ibid., Article 3(4): United Nations Political Officer of Somalia (UNPOS).

26 M Celestine, *Promoting the human rights of women in Kenya: a comparative review of the domestic laws*, Kenya, Nairobi: UNIFEM, 2010, 14.

27 Ibid.

28 Kenya's Independence Constitution, Section 82(1) and (3). Kenya Law Reform Reports: Republic of Kenya.

29 M Celestine, *Promoting the human rights of women in Kenya: a comparative review of the domestic laws*, Kenya, Nairobi: UNIFEM, 2010.

30 Ibid.

31 Personal laws are laws based on customs and religions, and are mostly patriarchal.

32 N Baraza, Family law reforms in Kenya: an overview, paper presented at the Heinrich Böll Foundation's Gender Forum in Nairobi, 30 April 2009.

33 Ibid, 1.

34 Constitution of Kenya 2010, Article 27. Kenya Law Reform Reports: Republic of Kenya.

35 Ibid., Article 24(4). Kenya Law Reform Reports: Republic of Kenya.

36 Ibid., Article 170(5). Kenya Law Reform Reports: Republic of Kenya.

37 UNIFEM, Kenya's Constitution of 2010: enhanced prospects for gender equality? UNIFEM/UN-WOMEN, 2010.

38 Ibid.

39 L Ochieng, Kenya passes controversial polygamy law, legislation condemned as a major setback for women, *Institute for War and Peace Reporting*, 2 May 2014, http://iwpr.net/global-voices/kenya-passes-controversial-polygamy-law

40 Constitution of Kenya 2010, Article 53. Kenya Law Reports. Republic of Kenya.

41 Ibid., Article 68c(iii). Kenya Law Reform Reports. Republic of Kenya.

42 J Chigiti, Kenya – a wife's right to matrimonial property, *The Star*, 3 April 2013, http://allafrica.com/stories/201304031413.html

43 Matrimonial Property Act 2013, (Section 2), Nairobi. Republic of Kenya.

44 Ibid., (Section 8), Nairobi. Republic of Kenya.

45 Ibid., (Section 12), Nairobi. Republic of Kenya.

46 Constitution of Kenya 2010, Article 48. Kenya Law Reform Reports. Republic of Kenya.

47 Ibid., Articles 28 and 29. Kenya Law Reform Reports. Republic of Kenya.

48 UNIFEM, Kenya's Constitution of 2010: enhanced prospects for gender equality?, 21, UNIFEM/UN-WOMEN, 2010.

49 Constitution of Kenya 2010, Article 21(3). Kenya Law Reform Reports. Republic of Kenya.

50 Provisional Constitution of the Federal Republic of Somalia, Article 11: United Nations Political Officer of Somalia (UNPOS).

51 Ibid., Article 24(5): United Nations Political Officer of Somalia (UNPOS).

52 Ibid., Articles 27(5) and 10(2): United Nations Political Officer of Somalia (UNPOS).

53 Ibid., Article 40: United Nations Political Officer of Somalia (UNPOS).

54 Ibid., Article 28(5): United Nations Political Officer of Somalia (UNPOS).

55 Ibid., Article 29(8): United Nations Political Officer of Somalia (UNPOS).

56 P Kyalo, A reflection on the African traditional values of marriage and sexuality, *International Journal of Academic Research in Progressive Education and Development*, 1, 2012.

57 R Nuune, Forced marriage a way of life in Somali culture, *Somalia Report*, 28 May 2011, www.somaliareport.com/index.php/post/778

58 Provisional Constitution of the Federal Republic of Somalia, Article 15: United Nations Political Officer of Somalia (UNPOS).

59 Ibid., Article 31(1).

60 WHO, Female genital mutilation and other harmful practices: prevalence of FGM, www.who.int/reproductivehealth/topics/fgm/prevalence/en/, (accessed August 2015).

61 NHS Choices, Female genital mutilation, May 2014, www.nhs.uk/Conditions/female-genital-mutilation/Pages/Introduction.aspx, (accessed August 2015).

62 CREAW, Wife inheritance, a death sentence behind the mask of culture, www.creawkenya.org/pdf/2009/wife_inheritance.pdf, (accessed August 2015).

63 M Celestine, *Promoting the human rights of women in Kenya: a comparative review of the domestic laws*, Kenya, Nairobi: UNIFEM, 2010, 15.

64 Ibid.

65 Ibid.

66 Ibid.

67 Constitution of Kenya 2010, Articles 27(6), 27(8), and 100. Kenya Law Reform Reports. Republic of Kenya.

68 Republic of Kenya, Advisory opinion Nr. 2 of 2012, www.judiciary.go.ke/portal/assets/files/Rulings/Majority%20Decision-One%20Third%20Rule.pdf, (accessed August 2015).

69 UNIFEM, Kenya's Constitution of 2010: enhanced prospects for gender equality?. UNIFEM/UN-WOMEN, 2010

70 Constitution of Kenya 2010, Article 81(b). Kenya Law Reform Reports. Republic of Kenya.

71 Ibid., Article 98(1). Kenya Law Reform Reports. Republic of Kenya.

72 Ibid., Article 97. Kenya Law Reform Reports. Republic of Kenya.

73 UNDP, Gender in Somalia, www.undp.org/content/dam/rbas/doc/Women's%20Empowerment/Gender_Somalia.pdf, (accessed August 2015).

74 Provisional Constitution of the Federal Republic of Somalia, Article 133. United Nations Political Officer of Somalia (UNPOS)

75 Ibid., Articles 3(5) and 38. United Nations Political Officer of Somalia (UNPOS).

76 J El-Bushra, Development and change: feminism, gender and women's peace activism, *International Institute of Social Studies*, 38, 2007.

77 G Stoppler, A rank usurpation of power – the role of patriarchal religion and culture in the subordination of women, *Duke Journal of Gender, Law and Policy*, 15, 2008, 365.

78 SL Monagan, Patriarchy: perpetuating the practice of female genital mutilation, *Journal of Alternative Perspectives in the Social Sciences*, 2, 2010.

79 S Ray, Understanding patriarchy, University of Delhi, www.academia.edu/4995045/Understanding_Patriarchy, (accessed August 2015).

80 N Igbelinna-Igbokwe, Africa: contextualizing gender based violence within patriarchy in Nigeria, *Pambazuka News*, 30 May 2013, allafrica.com/stories/201305311347.html

81 M Kambarami, Femininity, sexuality and culture: patriarchy and female subordination in Zimbabwe, 2006, www.arsrc.org/downloads/uhsss/kmabarami.pdf, (accessed August 2015).

82 C Kaimenyi, E Kinya, and S Macharia, An analysis of affirmative action: the two thirds gender rule in Kenya, *International Journal of Business, Humanities and Technology*, 3:6, 2013.

83 ML Krook, Reforming representation: the diffusion of candidate gender quotas worldwide, paper presented at the International Studies Association Annual International Convention, Montreal, Canada, 17–20 March 2004.

84 D Dahlerup, No quota fever in Europe?, paper presented at the International Institute for Democracy and Electoral Assistance (IDEA)/CEE Network for Gender Issues Conference, Budapest, Hungary, 22–23 October 2004.

85 V Naidoo and M Kongolo, Has affirmative action reached South African women?, *Journal of International Women's Studies*, 6:1, 2004.

86 N Siqwana-Ndulo, Clash of mandates: traditional and gender constitutional provisions in South Africa, *Consultancy Africa Intelligence*, 2013, www.consultancyafrica.com/index.php?option=com_content&view=article&id=1252:clash-of-mandates-traditional-and-gender-constitutional-provisions-in-south-africa&catid=91:rights-in-focus&Itemid=296, (accessed August 2015).

87 P Andrews, Democracy stops at my front door: obstacles to gender equality in South Africa, *Loyola University International Law Review*, 5:1, 2007.

88 I Ndungu, Does the dominance of women in Rwanda's parliament signify real change?, Institute for Security Studies, 12 November 2013, www.issafrica.org/iss-today/does-the-dominance-of-women-in-rwandas-parliament-signify-real-change.

89 C Abdi, Convergence of civil war and the religious right: reimagining Somali women, *Signs: Journal of Women in Culture and Society*, 33, 2007.

90 K Njogu and E Orchardson-Mazrui, Gender inequality and women's rights in the Great Lakes: can culture contribute to women empowerment?, www.unesco.org/new/fileadmin/MULTIMEDIA/HQ/SHS/pdf/Culture-Womens-Empowerment.pdf, (accessed August 2015).

91 K Oyaro, MEDIA-KENYA: for a woman candidate, it's good to be a man, *Kenya Environmental and Political News Weblog*, 10 December 2007, http://kenvironews.wordpress.com/2007/12/10/media-kenya-for-a-woman-candidate-its-good-to-be-a-man

Index

policy decision makers 21–2
Policy Framework for Security Sector Reform (2011) 5
Political Parties Act (2007) 107
politically-motivated violence, levels of 71
Port Elizabeth Black Civic Organisation (PEBCO) 37
Port Elizabeth Women's Organisation (PEWO) 37
Port Elizabeth Youth Congress (PEYCO) 38
post-apartheid African National Congress (ANC) regime 110
post-Cold War conflicts: character of 19; gender equality in 17
post-structural feminism 64
Prevention of Domestic Violence Act (1998) 110
Promotion of Equality and Prevention of Unfair Discrimination Act (2000) 110
Protocol to the African Charter on Human and People's Rights on the Rights of Women in Africa 5, 86, 101
'protracted guerrilla war' 33

qualitative change, absence of 23–5

Rajoelina, Andry 85
rape 110
Recognition of Customary Marriages Act (1998) 110
Regional Economic Communities (RECs) 25
roadmap, adoption of 88
Rwanda, genocide in 19

Sachs, Carolyn 64
SADC see Southern African Development Community
SADC Protocol on Gender and Development of 2008 25
SADF see South African Defence Force
SDGEA see Solemn Declaration on Gender Equality in Africa
security discourse 18
security sector: in rights advocacy functions, women 74–5; unprofessional tendencies of 71
security sector institutions (SSIs) 79
security sector reform (SSR): Congolese women in 94; Organising Technical Committee on 87, 88; programming in post-conflict countries 7; in Zimbabwe see Zimbabwe, case study of gender and security sector reform in
Sen, Amartya 62
sexual and gender-based violence (SGBV) 5, 82, 91; addressing of 92–3; challenging harmful stereotypes of 91–2; Congolese women in security sector reform 94; problem of 2; problems and achievements in combatting impunity 93–4; women as 'second-class citizens' 94–5

sexual harassment policy 74
sexual violence 92
SGBV see sexual and gender-based violence
Shagari, Shehu 81
'Six Day War' 33
social-work-oriented policing 79
sociocultural capital 46–7
Solemn Declaration on Gender Equality in Africa (SDGEA) 5, 25
Somali culture, harmful cultural practice in 106
Somali National Army 45
Somalia: gender equality for women 109–11; Kenya and 101–3
'Somalia operation' (KDF) 46
South African Defence Force (SADF) 34
Southern Africa Development Community (SADC) Protocol on Gender and Development 1, 4, 71, 86, 88
Southern Africa Gender Protocol Alliance, 'Gender, Peace and Security' cluster of 87
Southern African Development Community (SADC) 1, 25; percentage of women in defence forces 12, **13**
space-clearing, discursive 57–60
SRC see Supreme Religious Council
SSIs see security sector institutions
SSR see Security Sector Reform
stable peace analysis 19
state security services, efficacy of 72
structural violence 5, 19
Sun City Accords 90
Supreme Religious Council (SRC) 111

TFC see Transitional Federal Charter
traditional African gender notions 44
traditional clan system 102
traditional Nigerian societies 78
traditional security paradigms 18–19
Transitional Federal Charter (TFC) 108

UDHR see Universal Declaration of Human Rights
Umkhonto weSizwe (MK) 34
UN Department of Peacekeeping Operations (DPKO) 11, 24
United Nations Commission on the Status of Women 100
United Nations Development Fund for Women (UNIFEM) 21
United Nations Development Programme (UNDP) 20, 86
United Nations Joint Human Rights Office (UNJHRO) 91, 93
United Nations Population Fund (UNFPA) 24, 86, 91
United Nations Security Council (UNSC) 7, 17